D0291876

WITHDRAWN FROM
KENT STATE UNIVERSITY LIBRARIES

AMERICA AND THE VIRGINIA DYNASTY 1800–1825

America and the
Virginia Dynasty 1800—1825

FON W. BOARDMAN, JR.

HENRY Z. WALCK, INC.   *New York*

For my favorite son-in-law
and his wife

Copyright © 1974 by Fon W. Boardman, Jr.
All rights reserved. ISBN: 0-8098-3117-1.
Library of Congress Catalog Card Number: 73-19250.
Printed in the United States of America.

Library of Congress Cataloging in Publication Data

Boardman, Fon Wyman, date
  America and the Virginia dynasty, 1800–1825.

  SUMMARY: Chronicles the quarter century period
of Jefferson's, Madison's, and Monroe's administrations,
an era of much change and growth in the United States.
    1. United States—History—1801-1809—Juvenile
literature. 2. United States—History—1809-1817—
Juvenile literature. 3. United States—History—
1817-1825—Juvenile literature. [1. United States—
History—1801-1809. 2. United States—History—
1809-1817. 3. United States—History—1817-1825]
I. Title.
E338.B62   973.4'6   73-19250
ISBN 0-8098-3117-1

Contents

1 New Century, New President

A LITTLE BEFORE NOON in Washington, D.C., on March 4, 1801, a lanky, simply dressed man left Conrad and McMunn's boarding-house, a short ways south of the Capitol, on foot and headed for that unfinished building. Accompanied by some members of Congress, friends and other supporters, Thomas Jefferson, nearing his fifty-eighth birthday, walked to the Senate Chamber, the only part of the Capitol yet completed, there to be inaugurated as the third president of the United States of America.

The simple ceremony included the new president's inaugural address, an address that remains one of the most memorable ever de-livered by an incoming chief executive. Unfortunately, Jefferson was an exceedingly poor public speaker, and even in the small cham-ber hardly anyone heard much of the speech. In printed form, how-ever, it was widely read and eagerly discussed.

Obviously conscious of the recent bitter election campaign in which he had won by a narrow margin, Jefferson urged that the na-tion "restore to social intercourse that harmony and affection without which liberty and even life itself are but dreary things." Looking ahead, he spoke of the United States, "the world's best hope," as "kindly separated by nature, and a wide ocean, from the exterminat-ing havoc of one quarter of the globe," and as "possessing a chosen country, with room enough for our descendants to the thousandth and thousandth generation." After noting other "blessings" of the new nation, the president remarked that "still one thing more" was needed: "a wise and frugal government, which shall restrain men from injuring one another, shall leave them otherwise free to regulate their own pursuits of industry and improvement, and shall not take from the mouth of labor the bread it has earned." Near the end, he modestly promised: "I advance with obedience to the work, ready to retire from it whenever you become sensible how much better choices it is in your power to make."

At the conclusion of the ceremony, Jefferson walked back to Conrad and McMunn's, where he had been staying since November. It was one of the best boardinghouses in the young capital city and Jefferson was fortunate enough to have a parlor as well as a bedroom. For this he paid $15 a week, meals included. He dined there on inauguration day, seated as usual at the foot of the table, farthest from the most prized seat near the fire. Jefferson did not move into the President's House until late March.

Washington, D.C., became the official seat of the Federal government in the summer of 1800. Splendid plans had been made for it while George Washington was president. Washington asked the French architect and engineer, Charles Pierre L'Enfant (1754–1825), who served in the Continental Army during the Revolution, to submit plans, and he did so in 1791. He antagonized Congress, however, and Jefferson, who took an active part in the project, didn't like him. The result was that he was dismissed in 1792. Even though his plan was approved in principle, Congress did not have the money necessary to carry it out.

In the early years of the century, Washington was in reality a desolate village in which no one stayed any longer than he could help. The population was only 3,200 people, and about 600 of these were slaves. The Capitol was far from finished and a temporary brick building for the use of the House of Representatives was under construction. The President's House—some called it the President's Palace—was also unfinished. (Although it was painted or whitewashed, it was not called the White House until some years later.) Near it were the only other two government buildings yet erected—The Treasury Building and the State, War and Navy Building, the latter not entirely completed.

The original design for the Capitol was the work of William Thornton (1759–1828), who was educated as a doctor. An all-around man, he was also a poet, a painter and an enthusiastic racer of horses. Born a British subject, Thornton came to America in 1787, and two years later won a competition to design a building for the Library Company of Philadelphia. His design for the Capitol received President Washington's approval and Thornton was in charge of the construction until 1802. Washington laid the cornerstone in 1793. The architect of the President's House was James Hoban (1762–1831), who was born in Ireland and came to the United States in 1789. He had charge of construction from 1792 to 1799, but when Jefferson moved in, the mansion was far from being an imposing or comfortable home for the nation's chief executive. The roof leaked, the bedrooms had not been painted and the East Room was not even plastered. The elegant staircase called for in the plans had not been built, nor had the grounds been landscaped at all.

Connecting the Capitol and the President's House was Pennsylvania Avenue, which had been hacked through the trees and swamp. It was unpaved and spotted with stumps and mud holes. There were a few private buildings and businesses, mostly huddled near the Capitol. These included several more boardinghouses, a tailor, a washerwoman, a printer, a grocery store and an oyster house. Gouverneur Morris, New York businessman and politician, remarked of early Washington that it was "the best city in the world for a *future* residence. We want nothing here but houses, cellars, kitchens, well-informed men, amiable women, and other little trifles of the kind to make our city perfect."

In this raw town in early 1801, Thomas Jefferson (1743–1826) took over the highest executive position in the government, thereby founding, as it turned out, the "Virginia Dynasty"—twenty-four consecutive years in which the presidency was held in turn by three eminent natives of the state of Virginia. Jefferson was educated at the College of William and Mary, studied law and by the time he was twenty-six was a member of the Virginia state legislature and an advocate of resistance to British rule. Since 1776, when he was thirty-three, he had been best known as the author of the Declaration of Independence, and to say that that authorship was his greatest single achievement is no reflection on his later illustrious career. During the Revolution he served a difficult term as governor of Virginia, became minister to France after the war and, under Washington, was the nation's first secretary of state. While he held this post the first division along party lines began to develop in American politics. Jefferson found himself at odds with some of the other leaders of the Revolution, such as Alexander Hamilton and John Adams.

Jefferson and those who thought as he did wanted a simple Federal government of limited power and activity. They also believed that the right to vote should be widespread. Hamilton and his supporters, on the other hand, favored a strong central government that encouraged business and banking. They were aristocratic in outlook and did not trust the common man.

As head of one faction, Jefferson was elected vice-president in 1796 when the electoral college system made the person receiving the second-highest number of votes vice-president even though he held different political beliefs from those of the man elected president.

Formal portraits show Jefferson as an urbane, intelligent gentleman, but in day-to-day appearance and conduct he gave a different impression. He was a bit over six-feet tall, with reddish hair and a somewhat awkward manner. A British diplomat said he looked like "a tall, large-boned farmer." He was often too casual in his dress for his exalted position—at least some officials and diplomats thought so—for he received visitors to his office in a well-worn coat and old slippers. Yet everyone except his worst enemies admired his modesty and gentleness, and found him a most entertaining conversationalist. He had guests to dinner almost every day at the White House and was something of a gourmet. His wine bill ran to $2,400 a year and he was an acknowledged expert on the subject. Some of his guests, however, especially foreign diplomats, were thrown into a frenzy because he refused to observe the usual social rules of arranging places at table according to protocol.

Jefferson knew Greek and Latin, spoke French and Italian, had some acquaintance with a number of American Indian languages, which were a hobby with him, was a statesman, a political philosopher, an architect, a horticulturist and a violinist. He loved horse racing, invented a number of gadgets, and improved the design of the farmers' plow. He was president of the American Philosophical Society, the most prestigious intellectual body in the land, from 1797 to 1815. Little wonder that more than a century and a half later another president, John F. Kennedy, on the occasion of a dinner for all the American Nobel Prize winners he could assemble, remarked that here was "the most extraordinary collection of talents . . . that has ever been assembled together at the White House, with the possible exception of when Thomas Jefferson dined alone."

Jefferson's father was a Virginia farmer, and all his life Jefferson bought and sold land, farmed and raised livestock. His personal life was centered on Monticello, his self-designed, lovely home near Charlottesville, Virginia, to which he returned as often as possible. In spite of his efforts to make agriculture pay, his open-handed way of life and financial problems kept him almost continually in difficulties, especially in his later years. His personal life was marked by misfortune also. He married in 1772, but his wife died only ten years later; four of the six children born to the Jeffersons died young; one of the two remaining daughters, to both of whom he was devoted, died after childbirth in 1804.

Thomas Jefferson is remembered as America's first true democrat, an unwavering believer in the common sense of the common people. He also thought that the American democratic experiment would succeed only if the nation remained primarily agricultural, with every man owning his own farm, or setting up as an artisan or craftsman. This, he believed, would make the average citizen economically independent, and thus immune to political domination by business and banking interests. For this reason Jefferson opposed laws or other governmental actions that would grant privileges to businessmen and financial interests at what he considered to be the expense of the majority of the people and a danger to democratic rule. Jefferson's views on economics and government, more radical in his time than they seem today, caused him to be labeled an enemy of private property—especially after he looked favorably on the French Revolution which seemed to some people to be pulling down all the pillars of a stable society. In practice, Jefferson had to modify his views somewhat. He came to realize that even such a democracy as he favored needed to encourage shipping and commerce, and even manufacturing and banking, if the needs of a growing society were to be met. He and Hamilton differed not on whether private property was a good thing, but on how Americans were to share and control that property.

Jefferson was also criticized for his religious beliefs and his espousal of the ideas of the Enlightenment. In religion he was a deist, which meant he believed in a god who required no formal worship. Supernatural revelation was not necessary to faith. In the intellectual and political world, his agreement with the ideas of the Enlightenment, or Age of Reason, of the eighteenth century meant that he endorsed a rational approach to social and economic problems and discarded such older ideas as belief in the divine right of kings and the authority of an official church. If men took a secular view of the world and put into practice what logic and reason told them was right and practical, continual progress toward a better world for all was possible. These advanced political, social and religious views resulted in strong, and at times vicious, attacks on Jefferson by conservatives.

In spite of these beliefs and the steps he took to support them even when they were unpopular, Jefferson remained a slave owner all his life although he recognized the system as an evil one, and looked forward to its end. His denunciation of the slave traffic in the draft of the Declaration of Independence had been deleted by a majority of his fellow delegates. He later proposed laws for Virginia that would have ameliorated the condition of the slaves and might have led eventually to emancipation. None of these proposals got very far and Jefferson apparently realized that, given the general climate of opinion at the time, there was no practical way to put an end to slavery. In other areas, such as religious freedom and education, his efforts bore fruit, particularly in the founding of the University of Virginia in 1819. The university was almost entirely his brainchild.

After he left the presidency in 1809, Jefferson devoted himself to his many interests. He was eventually reconciled with his old revolutionary comrade and later political enemy, John Adams of Massachusetts, and on July 4, 1826, fifty years after the adoption of the Declaration of Independence, these two illustrious Founding Fathers died within hours of each other.

North, south and west of the new capital and the new president lay the sixteen states of the young nation. Besides the original thirteen colonies that became states, Vermont (1791), Kentucky (1792) and Tennessee (1796) had been admitted to the union. The admission of the last two indicated how rapidly population was flowing westward over the Allegheny Mountains. The total population of the country was about 5,300,000, of whom almost 900,000 were slaves. (The population of the British Isles in this period was approximately 15,000,000; of France, 27,000,000.) Most of the people lived within fifty miles of the Atlantic coast, from Massachusetts to Georgia, but almost half a million had moved beyond the Alleghenies. Only about 300,000 Americans lived in towns of 2,500 population or more. Spread unevenly over more than 800,000 square miles, the people of America were mostly farmers, mostly native-born and more likely than not of English descent, although there were sizable numbers of citizens of German, Scotch-Irish, Welsh and Dutch descent, plus some Swedes, Swiss and French Huguenots.

By virtue of climate and geography, the nature and background of the people who had settled them and the original style of government, the states of the union showed as many differences as similarities. Forging a united nation out of what for upwards of 200 years had been separate colonies was further complicated by poor transportation and slow communication. A letter took about twenty days to travel the 1,000 miles or so from New England to Georgia.

New England, long-settled, comparatively crowded and with little good farmland, was losing energetic citizens to the western lands. New England retained its Puritan background in its religion and its social customs. Shipping, trading and banking kept many New Englanders prosperous, but the section was starting to lose the high position it once held. It felt the commercial competition of the Middle Atlantic states, especially New York and Pennsylvania. The latter was also the intellectual center of the nation, partly because of the general atmosphere of freedom that had existed ever since William Penn established his Quaker outpost in the New World, and partly because Philadelphia had been the home of the Continental Congress, the Constitutional Convention and the new Federal government for most of the years before it moved to Washington.

The southern states were already thought of as a section differing from the rest of the nation, largely because of the agricultural economy and slavery. Virginia had the largest population of any state, about 865,000 people, of whom approximately 350,000 were slaves. Virginia also held first place in the number of national leaders it had given the nation. Washington and Jefferson were the most prominent, but by no means the only statesmen of stature. Among their fellow Virginians were such men as Patrick Henry, James Madison and Richard Henry Lee. The state had almost no city life and was controlled by country gentlemen-farmers who thrived on law and politics. To the south, North Carolina represented a more democratic system, with fewer of its inhabitants either at the very top or the very bottom of the social and economic ladder. South Carolina, on the other hand, boasted America's most sophisticated style of living among its large land owners, and prided itself on its cultural activities.

The United States contained five cities that compared favorably in the qualities making up urban life with the cities of Europe, except for London and Paris. The largest of these was Philadelphia (population 69,000), which owed much to Benjamin Franklin who had contributed greatly to its civic pride and its intellectual life. New York (64,000) was the most rapidly growing of the five cities, with a thriving port and expanding banking and commercial activity. Baltimore (26,000) was also a leading commercial town. In an era when communication and transportation between the coast and the land west of the mountains were even more difficult than between north and south, Baltimore's location gave it the best connections with the west. Boston (25,000), once the largest city in America, had lost ground and was now venerable enough to resemble an old-fashioned English market town. In the south, Charleston (20,000) completed

the roster of American cities. Besides its importance as a cotton shipping port, it was also the center of a lively cultural life for a large
area.

This, then, was the United States of America as it entered its
thirteenth year as a nation under the Constitution. Although joined
in union by history and by the Revolution, the states and the people
were separated not only by distance, but also, as Thomas Jefferson
knew only too well, by deep political differences which had emerged
in the recent presidential election.

2 Jefferson and the Louisiana Purchase

WHEN JEFFERSON ASSUMED the duties of the chief executive, he and the nation were still shaken by the political crisis through which they had passed in the election of 1800. The Constitution had not served as expected. In addition, a bitter partisan dispute threatened the tranquility of the country. The dispute was between the outgoing administration of John Adams and Jefferson's new one, and it involved control of the judicial system.

The division of the country into two strongly opposed political parties, a thing not contemplated by the men who had written the Constitution only fourteen years before, started in President Washington's first administration of 1789–93. The president brought into his cabinet men of different points of view. Emerging as the leaders of the two dominant forces, as well as personifying the two divergent paths the nation might take, were Alexander Hamilton, the first secretary of the treasury, and Jefferson. Hamilton (1755–1804), born in the West Indies, served in combat in the Revolution and as aide-de-camp to Washington. He helped write the Constitution and then worked long and hard to secure its adoption. Hamilton wrote the majority of the eighty-eight *Federalist* essays, most of which first appeared in New York City newspapers in 1787–88. The essays were also published in book form and had considerable influence in securing support for ratification of the Constitution. The other contributors were James Madison and John Jay (1745–1829). Jay, a New York and active in the Continental Congress, was the first chief justice of the United States.

By the time Washington's first administration took office, Hamilton was ready with a conservatively sound plan for establishing the national finances, which were in poor shape as a result of the expenses of the Revolution and the absence of a central fiscal authority. Hamilton and his followers—who were the founders of the Federalist party—stood for a strong central government, a restricted suffrage, emphasis on the protection of property rights, the encouragement of manufacturing, and a pro-British foreign policy. The Federalists believed that rule by the well-to-do and well-educated was best for the country. They were urban-oriented and found most of their support in New England and among the business class of the cities.

Jefferson became the spokesman and leader of the Republican party (which bore no relation to the present-day Republican party and was sometimes known as the Democratic-Republican party). The Republicans—in contrast with their opponents—favored restrictions on the scope and power of the central government, a broad suffrage, protection of the small farmer and artisan, defense of civil rights, and a pro-French foreign policy. The Republicans appealed to the farmers, the urban workers and the agricultural economy of the South. Some conflicts of interest developed fairly early between the Republicans' northern and southern followers, and between the more conservative southern planters and merchants and the small farmers and western pioneers.

When the time came for the 1800 presidential election, the political battle lines were sharply drawn, as well as aggravated by various acts of the administration of President Adams. Adams stood for reelection as the Federalist candidate. By choice of a caucus of his party's members in Congress, Vice-President Jefferson was nominated to run a second time for the top office. Adams's running mate was Charles Cotesworth Pinckney (1746–1825) of South Carolina. Pinckney fought in the Revolution and was a delegate to the Constitutional Convention. Jefferson's running mate, as in 1796, was Aaron Burr (1756–1836) of New York. A brilliant and successful lawyer, Burr also fought valiantly in the Revolution. He had already held many political offices, including that of United States senator. His popularity and political talents made the Republican party by 1800 the stronger party in New York State, and so of pivotal importance to Jefferson's success.

As was the custom of the time, the presidential candidates themselves did not do any campaigning, but public meetings were held throughout the land, newspapers were strongly partisan on one side or the other, and pamphlets, some of them scurrilous, were widely distributed. This first presidential election in which party machines played a leading role was an extremely dirty one. Republican partisans said the Federalists wanted to turn the nation over to a small group of plutocrats and, ultimately, to set up a monarchy. The Federalists called Jefferson an atheist and worse. They predicted that if he were elected "the soil will be soaked with blood, and the nation black with crimes."

When the votes of the Electoral College were counted, the Republicans were clearly the victors, but the result revealed a serious defect in the Constitution. That document, in Article II, provided that each elector vote for two persons. The candidate with the most votes, providing it was a majority of the total number of electors, became president; the candidate with the second largest total became vice-president. The drafters of the Constitution had anticipated that the electors would vote as individuals, selecting the two candidates they thought best fitted for the two highest offices in the land. Now that electoral voting followed party lines, serious trouble arose. Jefferson received seventy-three electoral votes, a clear majority, but Burr also received seventy-three votes. Adams had sixty-five and Pinckney sixty-four. The Republican electors intended Jefferson to be president, but no steps had been taken to make sure he received at least one more vote than Burr. As a result, the election was thrown into the House of Representatives where, as the Constitution provided, each state would have one vote in choosing between Jefferson and Burr.

Most Federalists favored Burr and tried to elect him, although that was not what the people intended. Hamilton, however, who detested Burr and thought him dishonest, worked actively behind the scenes to secure Jefferson's election. Much as they differed on public policy, Hamilton respected Jefferson's abilities. Burr publicly professed support for Jefferson, but did nothing to take himself out of the race. Jefferson never forgave him for this. Some Federalists apparently went so far as to scheme to continue the deadlock, hoping that some excuse could be found to keep Adams in the presidency or to put some other Federalist in as chief executive. Some of Jefferson's supporters vowed to make him president by force if necessary, and rumors spread that armed men were gathering in Pennsylvania and Virginia for this purpose.

Beginning on February 11, the House took thirty-five ballots without breaking the deadlock. On the thirty-sixth ballot on February 17, scarcely more than two weeks before a new president was scheduled to be inaugurated, Jefferson received a majority of the votes, by states, when certain Federalists gave up their support of Burr.

In the end, then, power was peacefully transferred from one set of interests to another, a process that many people in America and Europe did not think possible. The American political system, in spite of this early crisis which had tested its devotion to democratic principles, compared most favorably with past experience in Europe. The result was in stark contrast to the recent French Revolution with its violent and bloody overthrow of one regime by another. Jefferson went out of his way in his inaugural address to offer an olive branch to his opponents. Deliberately using a small "r" and a small "f," he said: "We are all republicans; we are all federalists." He added:

> If there be any among us who wish to dissolve this Union or to change its republican form, let them stand undisturbed, as monuments of the safety with which error of opinion may be tolerated where reason is left free to combat it.

Extreme Federalists, however, continued to equate Jefferson with the devil. Most extreme of all was Fisher Ames (1758–1808), a sharp-witted New England lawyer and one-time member of Congress. His outlook on life was well summed up in one of his gentler remarks: "A change, though for the better, is always to be deplored by the generation in which it is effected." As concerned Jefferson and democracy, Ames called the latter "an illuminated hell," and said of the former that his election would result in "the loathsome steam of human victims offered in sacrifice." Even the relatively restrained John Adams slipped quietly out of Washington at 4 A.M. on inauguration day and headed for New England, because he could not bring himself to witness the taking over of the presidency by his rival. No matter what he did, Jefferson continued to arouse exaggerated reactions from his enemies. Two years later the editor of the *Port Folio* magazine, commenting on his administration, wrote:

> The first and warmest wish of my heart is that my country may be saved from the severest scourge that Heaven, in its wrath, inflicts on people—the reign of Democracy.

One result of the disputed election was the ratification in 1804, in time for the next presidential election, of the twelfth amendment to the Constitution. It provided that henceforth electors would vote separately for president and vice-president. The Constitution was not amended again for sixty-two years.

As time showed, the change from a Federalist to a Republican regime made less difference than either side had feared or hoped. Jefferson did not have it in him to be either a demagogue or a dictator. While some basic differences existed between parties and people, the people were for the most part, whether Federalists or Republicans, the same generation of patriots who had worked together for many desperate years and had faced many difficult problems together before independence was achieved. The Federal government was now settled in Washington, the finances of the nation were in good condition. The government bureaucracy was small and it was staffed almost entirely by Federalists. His supporters at once put pressure on Jefferson to find positions for loyal Republicans. Here he proceeded slowly.

To lead the two most important cabinet departments, Jefferson chose two unusually able men, James Madison at State and Albert Gallatin for the Treasury. Gallatin (1761–1849) was a native of Geneva, Switzerland, who came to the United States in 1780 and settled in Pennsylvania. A natural leader, eager to serve in public life, Gallatin was elected a United States senator in 1793 but was put out of his seat on the grounds, which the Federalists were happy to support, that he had not been an American citizen long enough to qualify. Two years later Gallatin was elected to the House of Representatives and shortly became the leader of the Jeffersonian forces there. Gallatin served brilliantly as secretary of the treasury for a dozen years.

When Gallatin took over the Treasury, the national debt was $82,000,000 and, with Jefferson's approval, he laid out a plan to pay it all off within sixteen years. During Jefferson's eight years in office, the debt was reduced to $57,000,000 in spite of some large expenses that were not anticipated in 1801. This was accomplished even though all internal taxes were repealed. A steady growth in receipts from the tariff on imports helped considerably. Gallatin accomplished a good deal in the way of economy by cutting down on expenditures for the army and navy, which opened him to criticism when the War of 1812 came along. He proposed spending only $1,900,000 a year on all the armed forces, which reduced the army to 3,000 men and made it necessary to lay up some navy frigates. Government expenses in other areas were modest in any event. The government had only three foreign missions to support—Great Britain, France and Spain. Gallatin and Madison collected salaries of $5,000 each, while Supreme Court justices were paid $3,500.

The Republicans were in full control of the executive branch and had majorities in both houses of Congress, but the Federalists retained firm control of the judiciary. Not a single Republican sat on the Federal bench in 1801. The outgoing party made sure, so it thought, of continued Federalist control by passing the Judiciary Act of 1801 in mid-February, less than three weeks before the Republicans were to take over the government. This act, which had its good points, provided for nineteen more judges, most of them to reside and serve in various districts around the country. This would eliminate the Supreme Court justices as circuit judges. Hitherto, the members of the highest court had had to travel around the country, as well as sit in Washington. President Adams showed no nonpartisan spirit in filling the new judicial positions and in appointing the numerous necessary aides. Every man named was a staunch Federalist, and three of the judges were appointed on the very last day of Adams's term, leading to unkind references to "midnight judges." The Federalists intended to "save" the nation and the Constitution by retaining control of the courts as a bulwark against Republican power in the executive and legislative branches.

The Republicans set about undoing the Federalist scheme and in March, 1802, passed a new judiciary act which, in effect, repealed the one of the year before, abolishing judgeships and making further changes in the system. Federalist orators once more proclaimed the death of the Constitution.

So far as the judiciary was concerned, Adams's most momentous act in the long run was to name John Marshall chief justice in late January, 1801. Marshall (1755–1835) was born in a log cabin in Virginia, the eldest of fifteen children. Through his mother, he was related to several well-known Virginia families such as the Lees, the Randolphs and the Jeffersons. After serving as an officer in the Revolution, Marshall became a lawyer, and like many Virginians of the time, a successful one. This led to his election to public office, including the House of Representatives and, in 1800, his appointment by President Adams as secretary of state.

Marshall remained chief justice of the United States until his death in 1835. During that long period, he asserted the power of the judicial branch in relation to other parts of the government. He established as a fundamental point of constitutional law that has never since been seriously questioned the right of the Supreme Court to declare laws passed by Congress unconstitutional. Marshall so dominated the court for over thirty-four years that only eight times did a majority of the court disagree with him. Of 1,100 decisions handed down, he wrote the majority opinion in 519 cases. Meanwhile, the more they opposed each other in political theory and practice, the more Marshall and Jefferson, both devoted to the new nation, came to dislike each other and to stand for two irreconcilable views concerning the nature of the American government. Marshall's favorable attitude toward a strong central government and his stern rule of the Supreme Court for so long have left an impression of an imperious, humorless autocrat of the judge's bench. In fact, Marshall was a tall, rather shambling man, usually carelessly dressed, who in the company of friends was convivial, relaxed and cheerful.

Marshall soon had an opportunity to use a particular and rather minor case as an excuse to assert wide authority for the Supreme Court. In *Marbury* vs. *Madison,* a man who had received a "midnight appointment" from Adams, as a justice of the peace in the District of Columbia, sued to force the new administration to deliver his actual commission which he had not received in the last-minute scramble of paperwork between administrations. By the time a decision was rendered in 1803, Chief Justice Marshall, who wrote the opinion of the court, sided with Marbury so far as his right to receive his commission, but found grounds for declaring that the law on which Marbury based his suit was unconstitutional. This was the first time that the Supreme Court had asserted its right to declare an act of Congress null and void, and it established that right once and for all. It was a little more than half a century before the Supreme Court again overruled an act of Congress.

In the meantime, Jefferson and the Republicans were not idle in their attempts to loosen the Federalist hold on the judiciary. On the grounds that Federalist judges were rendering opinions based on their political beliefs rather than the law, the Republicans sought to impeach some of their opponents. They saw no other way to make room for Republican judges. The most important case involved Samuel Chase (1741–1811), who had been appointed to the Supreme Court in 1796 and had been its leader in setting forth Federalist principles until Marshall ascended to the chief justiceship. A delegate to the Continental Congress, Chase helped put Maryland on the side of independence and was one of the signers of the Declaration. Although he opposed adoption of the Constitution, he soon came to be a thorough-going Federalist.

On the highest court, Chase became increasingly arrogant and high-handed. He lectured juries on the evils of democracy, and, to put it mildly, showed a lack of judicial temperament and objectivity. The Republicans—seeing an opportunity to attack the Federalist judges—mustered enough strength in the House of Representatives to vote a bill of impeachment in December, 1804, on charges of malfeasance, alleging bias on Chase's part in two recent trials of Republican partisans. The Senate, with some Republican support, refused to convict Chase. The Republicans abandoned any further attempt to purge the judiciary of Federalists by impeachment, even though individuals such as Justice Chase deserved some kind of chastisement.

The prolonged suspense of the presidential election and the sharp battle between the executive and the judicial branches both fade into the background today in comparison with the events surrounding the Louisiana Purchase of 1803. When Jefferson took office, the nation's western boundary was the Mississippi River, while to the south Florida belonged to Spain. Beyond the great river, Spain also held title to a large stretch to the north and west known as Louisiana, while to the southwest lay Texas, Mexico and other territories, all part of New Spain. Before her defeat in the Seven Years War France had ruled Louisiana, which French trappers and Jesuit missionaries had explored and had settled, although very sparsely except for the cosmopolitan city of New Orleans near the mouth of the Mississippi.

In October, 1800, Spain, pressured by France's new supreme ruler, Napoleon Bonaparte, secretly retroceded Louisiana to France. Napoleon had dreams of reestablishing France's empire in the New World, which had been lost in 1763, and any move in this direction would be a blow against his chief enemy, Great Britain. Jefferson learned of the secret treaty in May, 1801, and was at once alarmed. Americans west of the Allegheny Mountains depended at that time on the western rivers, which flowed into the Mississippi, and on the Mississippi itself, for transporting their agricultural products. New Orleans was as important to the United States as any port on the Atlantic coast and a treaty with Spain allowed Americans the right of deposit there. This meant they could land their goods without paying any duty until the goods were further transshipped. Much as he had once admired the French Revolution, Jefferson had no illusions about the ambitions of Napoleon and, as he wrote to one of his diplomatic agents, if France occupied New Orleans, "We must marry ourselves to the British fleet and nation," in self-protection. Jefferson and others were further alarmed in the fall of 1802 when Spain suddenly revoked the right of deposit in spite of the treaty. Fortunately, the right was restored in the spring of 1803.

Jefferson sought and secured from Congress $2,000,000 to offer to France for New Orleans and West Florida, although no one was sure whether the latter was part of Louisiana or not. Napoleon, in the meantime, was having second thoughts about Louisiana. He had sent a strong force to Santo Domingo, in the West Indies, early in 1802 to try to subdue François Toussaint L'Ouverture, a former slave who had led a successful rebellion there. Strong resistance by the Black revolutionists, together with yellow fever, virtually wiped out the French army, including its commanding general. Without control of Santo Domingo, Louisiana was of little value to France. On the one hand, Santo Domingo was a military and naval base that could be used to protect the approaches to the mouth of the Mississippi River from British or other invasion forces. On the other hand, one of the chief values of Louisiana in the days of French rule of the prosperous colony of Santo Domingo had been to supply that colony with food and other goods. Finally, war with Great Britain was certain to start up again in the near future and Napoleon needed money to finance it.

In April, 1803, a surprised American minister in Paris was asked what his country would pay for all of Louisiana. With no legal authority to commit the United States, American representatives in a little more than two weeks of negotiations, agreed to pay about $15,000,000 for Louisiana. A quarter of this was to be used to pay debts owed by France to certain American citizens.

Back home this real-estate deal caused a crisis both of constitutional law and conscience for Jefferson. From the Republican point of view of limited powers of the central government, nothing in the Constitution sanctioned the purchase of territory from a foreign power. Jefferson at first held out for an amendment to legalize the purchase, but as a practical matter he soon dropped the idea. He feared that Napoleon would change his mind and he knew that the nation highly approved of this grand geographical coup that would give the whole long, broad Mississippi River to the eager farmers, traders and boatmen who were settling the western territory. A few disgruntled Federalists, who normally would have defended the power of the Federal government to do almost anything, cried that the transaction was unconstitutional. One Federalist senator declared: "I believe it will be the greatest curse that could at present befall us."

Congress voted the money and the authority and on December 20, 1803, France formally surrendered Louisiana to the United States in a flag-raising ceremony in New Orleans. The geographical extent of the nation was thereby doubled, since Louisiana consisted of about 828,000 square miles, although no one knew its exact boundaries. The cost was about four cents an acre and eventually thirteen states were created out of its vast reaches. It was mostly an unknown, even frightening, land. Some said there was a large, active volcano up the Missouri River. Another rumor had it that there existed a mountain of solid salt, 180 miles long and 45 miles wide. This led a jealous Federalist editor to suggest that perhaps there was also "an immense lake of molasses and . . . a vale of hasty pudding, stretching as far as the eye could reach."

But the land was there, many Americans were eager to make use of it, and it is impossible to imagine Jefferson, the Congress and the people not seizing such a once-in-history opportunity.

3 Jefferson and the Burr Conspiracy

JEFFERSON'S POPULARITY, thanks largely to the Louisiana Purchase, was high at the time of the 1804 presidential election. Jefferson and the Republicans would certainly sweep the field against a badly disorganized Federalist party. Burr, out of favor with Jefferson and others of the party, was dropped as vice-president. Jefferson's new running mate was George Clinton (1739–1812) of New York, and his selection was a direct slap at Burr since the Clinton family was in rivalry with Burr for the leadership of the New York Republicans.

Clinton served in the Continental Congress and as a brigadier general during the Revolution. Elected governor of New York in 1777, he provided such popular and able leadership that he was reelected five consecutive times. Clinton actively opposed ratification of the Constitution because he thought it took too much power away from the states, and he wrote some carefully thought out public letters on the subject. The Federalists put up for the presidency Charles Cotesworth Pinckney, who had been Adams's running mate four years before. On the ticket for vice-president was Rufus King (1755–1827), born in Maine when it was part of Massachusetts. A delegate to the Constitutional Convention, he was a strong supporter of that body's work. Moving to New York, he became one of the state's first two United States senators.

The result in the Electoral College was one-sided. With seventeen states now voting (Ohio was admitted in 1803, the first state in the old Northwest Territory), Jefferson and Clinton received 162 electoral votes to 14 for Pinckney and King. The Republicans lost only Connecticut and Delaware, plus two of Maryland's votes. They carried the one-time stronghold of Federalism, Massachusetts, and also retained control of the Senate and the House.

The nation's foreign relations had been generally peaceful and satisfactory during Jefferson's first term, capped, of course, by the Louisiana Purchase. Although the end of the struggle between Great Britain and Napoleonic France was not in sight, the two nations were on the verge of a short period of peace late in 1801. A Franco-American agreement cancelled some older treaties and settled other problems, such as certain claims for payments of debts, while in the spring of 1802, the United States and Great Britain satisfactorily concluded negotiations concerning private American debts owed to British creditors.

In the very first year of Jefferson's second term, however, conditions changed. Napoleon, who had recently crowned himself emperor, was again at war with a coalition headed by Great Britain. For either side to win a decisive and final victory seemed almost impossible. Napoleon had the greater strength on land and dominated the continent. The British navy was supreme at sea. Both sides tried to prevent neutral shipping from carrying goods to the enemy. Since the United States had by far the largest merchant marine of any neutral nation, and since Great Britain had the most warships, a clash of interests, if not of naval power, was inevitable.

The British not only claimed the right to search merchant ships and seize cargo they considered contraband—especially if it was a product of an enemy country or colony—but they also used their power to take from neutral ships crewmen they claimed were British subjects. This issue of "impressment" created bad feeling between the United States and Great Britain at a time when the old antagonisms of the revolutionary period were dying out. British seamen deserted steadily to the American navy and merchant marine. The pay and living conditions were better, and the treatment received from superior officers was much less harsh. Between the Revolution and the War of 1812 about 20,000 British seamen deserted to the United States. Many of them became naturalized American citizens, but Great Britain refused to acknowledge the right of Britons to abandon their nationality. Furthermore, with Americans and Britons speaking the same language and looking and dressing much alike, to tell one from another was difficult. In the period from 1803 to 1805, more than 2,000 Americans were unjustly impressed by ships of the British fleet.

The issue came to a head on June 22, 1807, a few miles off the Virginia coast, when the British navy frigate *Leopard* hailed the American navy frigate *Chesapeake* and demanded to be allowed to send a search party aboard to look for a particular British deserter. The commander of the *Chesapeake*, Commodore James Barron, refused, whereupon the *Leopard* fired a broadside into the unprepared American ship, killing three Americans and wounding eighteen. Barron was forced to surrender and the British took off not only the deserter, whose true identity was not known to the American captain, but also three American citizens.

The nation was outraged by this incident and if Jefferson had said the word, war would have been declared against Great Britain at once. Jefferson, however, did not want war. In the first place, he believed as a matter of principle that disputes between nations should be settled by peaceful means. Secondly, as a practical matter, he believed that the British needed the food and other products being carried in American ships so badly that if the United States threatened to withhold its commerce, Britain would back down on impressment and other disputed issues. Thus economic pressure would be a substitute for war.

In the meantime, in the spring of 1806, Great Britain proclaimed a blockade of the European coast from Brest to the Elbe River. Napoleon retaliated in the fall by declaring the British Isles blockaded. Jefferson's first move was to sponsor the Non-Importation Act of 1806 which forbade the importation of certain specified British goods. This failed to impress the British. In December, 1807, another step was taken with the passage by Congress of the Embargo Act which prohibited all American vessels from sailing to any foreign port, and forbade foreign ships from taking on cargo in American ports. The British remained unmoved while Napoleon cynically seized all the American ships he could on the grounds that, if they really were American craft, he was helping Jefferson enforce the embargo; or, since American ships were forbidden to sail, they must be British ships unlawfully flying the American flag.

Jefferson's theory that economic pressure would force the British to meet American demands did not work out in practice, although there is a possibility that if the embargo had been carried on for a longer time and if it could have been completely enforced, it would have had the desired effect. However, ships could not be kept from sneaking out of harbor, while the United States–Canadian border provided innumerable opportunities for smuggling in both directions. The embargo failed in part because those whom it was supposed to help—the shipowners and the producers of export goods—did not want to be "helped" in this way. Despite the loss of many ships and cargoes to the warring European nations, America's foreign trade was highly profitable because the war inflated the demand for shipping and for goods produced in America and in the colonies of the European nations. Britain felt the pinch less than expected because she was able to increase her trade with Latin America.

Jefferson's popularity declined rapidly. New England voted Federalist again. Many Republicans, especially those in the South and other agricultural areas, turned against their leader because they could not sell their goods. Thousands of sailors were idle. Some merchants, unable to use their capital in the normal avenues of commerce and shipping, turned to manufacturing, so that the embargo was the indirect cause of the nation's first serious steps into the industrial world, especially in the textile field.

Jefferson had to admit defeat by early 1809, and on March 1, just three days before his second term expired, he accepted repeal of the Embargo Act. A Non-Intercourse Act took its place. This new law permitted the resumption of trading with all countries except France and Great Britain. The president was empowered to reopen trade with either or both of the offending powers if they repealed their edicts aimed at American shipping.

In domestic affairs, also, Jefferson had an unhappy experience in his second term, involving Aaron Burr and charges of treason. Knowing he would not be nominated for the vice-presidency in 1804, Burr ran for governor of New York as an independent Republican and was supported by most Federalists as a blow against Jefferson. Alexander Hamilton, however, not only refused to support Burr but worked actively against him. When Burr lost in a close race, he blamed Hamilton, and the enmity between the two set the stage for one of the great tragedies of American public life.

Burr heard that Hamilton had called him "a dangerous man, and one who ought not to be trusted with the reins of government," and that he had referred to him as a "despicable person." Burr demanded an explanation, and when Hamilton did not give him a straightforward answer, he challenged him to a duel. Hamilton reluctantly accepted and early on the morning of July 11, 1804, the antagonists, their seconds and a doctor rowed across the Hudson to Weehawken, New Jersey. Hamilton resolved not to try to shoot Burr, but Burr was in earnest. Hamilton fell mortally wounded and died thirty-one hours later. Dueling was an accepted method of settling disputes between American gentlemen in the first half of the nineteenth century, and such men as Henry Clay and Andrew Jackson fought duels. Nevertheless, the public outcry against the controversial Burr for having killed one of the leading soldiers and statesmen of the land was great. New Jersey indicted him for murder. Burr fled to Philadelphia and then to Georgia, but in November he turned up in Washington and presided over the Senate as vice-president as though nothing had happened.

Burr's chances for a further career in public office had vanished, but not his restless ambition. His attention turned westward, especially to the lower Mississippi area and the Spanish possessions farther west. Rumors spread of schemes involving intrigues against Spain. Burr conferred secretly with General James Wilkinson (1757–1825) who was governor of Louisiana Territory in 1805–06. Wilkinson was perhaps the most unsavory scoundrel ever to wear the uniform of the United States Army. In his earlier career he was involved in several episodes in which his conduct was irregular, but no serious punishment was meted out. During the Revolution, he had been entrusted with taking the official report of the American victory at Saratoga to the Continental Congress. He was so slow in arriving that the Congress censured him—but nevertheless promoted him to brigadier general. By the time he became involved with Burr, he had some years before secretly taken an oath of allegiance to Spain and was in that country's pay, so that he was a spy against his own country. However, at this time he was still the ranking officer in the United States Army.

Burr was also in touch with the British minister to the United States. Perhaps he intended to separate the trans-Allegheny west from the rest of the country and make it an independent country with Britain's blessing. Perhaps he planned to separate only the New Orleans area from the United States. Another story had it that he was going to seize Texas and other Spanish territory for the United States. Or, possibly, his eye was on Mexico, which he and his followers would conquer and then make Burr the ruler of that nation. Burr had a great deal of charm and attracted many people to his side. In the spring of 1805 he began a trip down the Ohio River that focused attention on him.

Stopping overnight at Blennerhassett Island in the Ohio near Parkersburg, Virginia, he found a strong supporter in the man for whom the island was named. Harman Blennerhassett (1765–1831) was a wealthy Irishman who had come to the United States in 1796, in effect having been driven from Ireland because he had married his beautiful niece. He bought part of the island and built a mansion there, along with a laboratory where he performed experiments in physics.

Burr reached Nashville, Tennessee, in late May, where Andrew Jackson, among other prominent citizens, made him welcome. A month later, he was greeted as a hero in New Orleans. Burr returned east, convinced that he could raise enough support to carry out whatever scheme he had in mind. He started west again in August, 1806, picking up some recruits at Pittsburgh, and then proceeding to Blennerhassett Island where his friend had mortgaged his island to help him. Apparently the two did some wild talking, which was overheard and circulated, adding to the rumors sweeping the country.

Burr was again dealing with Wilkinson, and in July wrote a letter to him in cipher, which Wilkinson later altered to serve his own purposes. In late October, Wilkinson got cold feet and decided to save his neck at the expense of his fellow plotter. He wrote President Jefferson, denouncing Burr and mentioning "a deep, dark, wicked, and widespread conspiracy," without, of course, admitting he was a part of it. Seriously alarmed by now, Jefferson issued a proclamation which did not mention Burr by name but warned of a "criminal enterprise," told all involved to desist, and instructed authorities in the various states to take action. In Ohio officials seized

some boats being built for Burr, and militia forces invaded Blennerhassett Island seeking conspirators.

Burr himself left Nashville on December 22, with two unarmed
boats and a few followers. Blennerhassett joined Burr, who then
learned how seriously he was in trouble, although he did not yet
know that the villainous Wilkinson had betrayed him. By now Burr's
company consisted of nine boats and about sixty men. On January
17, 1807, Burr decided it was best if he gave himself up to the civil
authorities in Mississippi Territory, which he did. He then became
alarmed as to what might befall him if people such as Wilkinson
caught up with him, so he fled on horseback and in disguise. He was
soon recognized, taken captive by the military and placed under ar-
rest for the long trip to Richmond, Virginia, where he was to stand
trial for treason against the United States of America.

Richmond was the scene of the trial because Blennerhassett
Island was a part of Virginia and presumably that was where Burr
had committed treason while making his plans. Richmond as the
trial scene also meant that Chief Justice Marshall would preside.
Crowds flocked to Richmond for the trial and the other legal ma-
neuvers which went on all summer. Both Burr and the government
were represented by the most able lawyers of the time. In effect,
though, the prosecution was run by Jefferson from the White House,
for he was determined that Burr be penalized. The trial, therefore,
was also a new confrontation between two great enemies, Marshall
and Jefferson.

The lawyers spent many hours in legal argument. The star witness was General Wilkinson, who made a sorry impression compared
with the handsome and dignified Burr, and was disliked by almost
everyone. His testimony was not impressive, no doubt because he ran
a very real risk of being tried for treason himself if he told the whole
truth about the part he had played. At one point, Burr requested
that Justice Marshall issue a subpoena ordering Jefferson to turn

General Wilkinson's letter and other papers over to the court. Jefferson announced that as president he must reserve the right to decide what papers should be made public, but that he would authorize the prosecution's lawyers to produce the letter, except for parts he did not consider material. On the same day, Marshall ordered a subpoena served on the president, but the issue was not pressed to a showdown.

Article III of the Constitution specifies that treason against the United States "shall consist only in levying War against them, or in adhering to their Enemies, giving them Aid and Comfort." Also, no person can be convicted, short of confession, unless two witnesses testify to the same "overt Act." Justice Marshall ruled that there had been no "overt Act" and that in any event there were not two witnesses to whatever acts had taken place. On this statement of the law, the jury had no choice but to acquit Burr of treason against his country.

Burr went into exile in Europe in June, 1808. He hatched various plans and schemes, but found few people in the several countries he journeyed to who were anxious to deal with him. He was in financial difficulties, too. By 1812, Burr felt it safe to return to America, which he did under an assumed name. He soon resumed the practice of law, with some success, but tragedy pursued him. From South Carolina came word from his daughter that his young grandson, of whom he had made so much, was dead. The child's mother was Theodosia Burr Alston, beautiful and talented and in her early years the focus of Burr's life. Theodosia's mother died when she was small and, from the age of eleven, the precocious girl had been her father's hostess in the glittering New York mansion where Burr delighted to play the grand host. At eighteen Theodosia married Joseph Alston, who later became governor of South Carolina.

Theodosia, scarcely thirty, was seriously ill of cancer, but she was determined to see her father once more now that he had returned to America. She set forth from Charleston aboard a fast ship on Decem-

ber 30, 1812. The ship disappeared in a raging storm off Cape Hat-
teras and Theodosia was never heard of again. Later, when he was
seventy-seven years old, Burr wed a well-to-do New York widow, but
it was not a happy affair. She sued for divorce and the decree became
final on the day Burr died, September 14, 1836.

Jefferson announced in December, 1807, more than a year before
his second term expired, that he would not run again. In spite of his
troubles over the embargo and the furor over the Burr conspiracy, he
probably could have won a third term had he cared to try. When
inauguration day, March 4, 1809, came, Jefferson declined the in-
vitation of his successor, James Madison, to ride in his carriage to
the ceremony. He did not think the new president should have to
share the honors of the day with the outgoing chief executive. Jefferson rode to the Capitol on horseback, unattended. He dined later
with only his young grandson for company, and in the evening the
nearly sixty-six-year-old Jefferson went to the inaugural ball. When
he arrived he asked: "Am I too early? You must tell me how to be-
have, for it is more than forty years since I have been to a ball." He
was shortly off to Monticello, to be with his books and to look after
his 10,000 acres of land and 200 slaves.

The author of the definitive biography of Thomas Jefferson,
Dumas Malone, sums up the Jefferson regime:

> One cannot speak with full assurance in such a matter, but it would
> appear that he presided over the most tolerant government on earth
> and the most democratic society. There was nothing comparable in
> the chief nations of Europe at any rate.

4   Madison and War

EARLY IN 1808 the Republicans in congressional caucus nominated
Jefferson's secretary of state, James Madison, for the presidency.
George Clinton was renominated for vice-president. The Republicans were much stronger than the Federalists but were splitting into
factions. As a result, anti-embargo Republicans in New York backed
Clinton for president, while in the South Republicans who felt Jefferson had deserted their principles named James Monroe. The latter, however, declined to be a candidate. The Federalists' candidate
was Charles Cotesworth Pinckney, who had been their candidate four
years before. In spite of the Republican split, Madison won easily,
receiving 122 electoral votes to 47 for Pinckney, and 6 for Clinton.
For the vice-presidency the electors gave a majority to Clinton.

Like Jefferson, James Madison (1751–1836) was a Virginian, although he was educated at the College of New Jersey (Princeton)
rather than William and Mary College. An anti-British patriot from
the start, Madison served in the Continental Congress where in 1780
he was the youngest delegate, but it was at the Constitutional Convention of 1787 that he first became prominent. His mastery of political science and his skill in logical argument made him the center
of the process of drafting a constitution. He ranks nearer to being
the "father" of the Constitution than any other one man. As a member of the House of Representatives in the first Congress he strongly

supported the ratification of the first ten amendments to the Constitution—the Bill of Rights. When Jefferson and the Republicans won the election of 1800, Madison was a logical and wise choice for secretary of state. In this office he proved to be an able diplomat, while operating the department with a staff of one chief clerk and six other clerks. As president, he would now be executing policies he had helped establish.

While Madison was worthy of the title of statesman, he had little talent for day-to-day administration. Nor was he adept as a politician, since his personality was not the kind that charms the public. A small, slender man, five feet, six inches tall, he was a neat dresser, quiet and seemingly cold in company, although he loosened up among friends. Madison's wife, a widow seventeen years younger whom he married in 1794, was a fortunate contrast to the new president. Dolley Payne Madison (1768–1849) was a lively, outgoing woman, with black hair and blue eyes. The author Washington Irving described her as "a fine portly, buxom dame, who has à smile and a pleasant word for everybody." Mrs. Madison loved to entertain and her evening levees at the White House became the most popular events of Washington's social life. When Congress appropriated $26,000 in 1809 to refurbish the White House, Mrs. Madison made sure the architect set aside $458 of it to buy a pianoforte she much desired.

The struggle between France on one side and Great Britain and most of Europe on the other went on almost continually during Madison's first four years in office. The contest included economic warfare as well as land and sea battles, with the United States remaining caught in the middle so far as maritime trade was concerned. Madison in his inaugural address made it clear that he would continue Jefferson's policy of peaceful coercion against Great Britain and France, using the Non-Intercourse Act which became law a few days before he became chief executive.

In May, 1809, the British minister in Washington informed

Madison that his country would exempt the United States from its wartime rules concerning ocean commerce if Madison would continue the American restrictions on trading with France. Madison accepted this deal and in June 600 vessels left American ports with full cargoes. Within weeks, however, word came from England that the foreign secretary had repudiated his minister's actions. After some hesitation, Madison again put the Non-Intercourse Act into effect against Great Britain. Once more the administration was assailed by its political enemies and by those who wanted to be able to sail the seas.

Congress reacted by passing in the spring of 1810 Macon's Bill No. 2, named for a congressman. This rather ingenious law permitted normal commercial relations with any nation. If, however, either Great Britain or France acknowledged the neutral rights America claimed, the latter would shut off trade with the nation still harassing United States commerce.

Napoleon promptly made use of this new law to trick Madison's administration. He informed the United States in August that on November 1, his restrictions on American shipping would be lifted and that he assumed an embargo would be ordered against trading with Great Britain unless it, too, eased its restrictions. In the form in which Madison received the French emperor's message, he was led to believe that Napoleon had already acted and so he announced that the British embargo would be restored. Britain protested, rightly, that Napoleon had not in fact kept his word.

America's well-meaning attempts to avoid war by embargoing foreign trade were not working. The failure of the embargo policy and the impressment of American seamen, which remained a sore point with many who felt it an insult to the nation's honor, increased the general ill will toward Great Britain and contributed to a growing demand for war. In addition, some leaders, especially those from the West and South, saw such a war as an opportunity to rid the West of British influence over the Indians there. Many believed that this influence had been used deliberately to arouse the Indians against American settlers. Others hoped to expand the United States by conquering some or all of Canada and Florida.

Madison sent a war message to Congress on June 1, 1812, which, after listing the reasons for armed conflict, said, in the language of official papers of the time:

> Whether the United States shall continue passive under these progressive usurpations and these accumulating wrongs, or, opposing force to force in defense of their national rights, shall commit a just cause into the hands of the Almighty Disposer of Events . . . is a solemn question which the Constitution wisely confides to the legislative department of the government.

Congress voted for war and Madison signed the declaration on June 18, but the balloting hinted that the country was far from unanimous in wanting war. The House approved by seventy-nine to forty-nine, the Senate by only nineteen to thirteen. Five days later, the British government revoked its orders against neutral commerce but word could not cross the Atlantic until too late.

The vote on the declaration of war followed both political and geographical lines. The Federalists, who were strongest in New England, were anti-Republican, pro-British and wanted no part in what they came to call sneeringly "Mr. Madison's War." Nor were the shipping interests, including those of the middle states who were supposedly being defended, anxious for a war which they believed would do them more harm than good. But along the frontier and in the South, where Republicanism was strong, where there was anti-British sentiment and where men hoped to enlarge the territory of the nation, the vote was for war.

The pro-war faction was led by a group of young "War Hawks," most of them quite new members of Congress and none of them over forty. Among them were two men who played important parts in public life until the middle of the century: Henry Clay (1777–1852) and John C. Calhoun (1782–1850). Clay was born in Virginia, studied law as a young man, moved to Lexington, Kentucky, in 1797, and was active in politics and as a legislator. Sent to the United States Senate to fill a short term in 1810, he had been seated only two weeks when he delivered a speech on war and patriotism in which he declaimed:

> I trust I shall not be deemed presumptuous when I state that I verily believe that the militia of Kentucky are alone competent to place Montreal and Upper Canada at your feet.

Clay was elected to the House of Representatives the next year and that body immediately named him the speaker, a post which he made much more influential than it had been. Calhoun, whose paternal grandmother was killed by Indians in 1760, was born in South Carolina and made his long and distinguished career there. He started out as a nationalist and ended as a defender of states rights and the Southern way of life. Calhoun entered Congress in 1810 when he was twenty-eight years old.

Soon after the nation went to war, the time came for another presidential election and the results reflected the opposition of many of the voters to armed conflict with Great Britain. Madison was renominated by the Republican party, but anti-war Republicans put up De Witt Clinton (1769–1828) to oppose him, and the Federalists endorsed Clinton. Clinton was a nephew of George Clinton and held many public offices, including that of United States senator, and was mayor of New York for a total of ten one-year terms between 1803 and 1815. Madison was reelected, but by an electoral vote of only 128 to 89. He lost every state north of the Potomac River except Vermont and Pennsylvania.

Neither the army nor the navy was in any condition to fight a war against one of the two superpowers of the time, although Great

Britain was so occupied battling Napoleon that it was unlikely to bring major forces to America if it could be avoided. On the American side, the unpopularity of the war in many quarters made it difficult for the administration to wage war efficiently. Congress voted a bill to add 25,000 men to the regular army, but everyone doubted, rightly, that this many volunteers would ever come forward. The army in 1812 consisted of 6,744 men, scattered among twenty-three posts and forts all over the country. The militia of some states was of no help because anti-war governors refused to allow their troops to serve outside the state. The navy, although superior to the army in quality, was small, especially compared with the British navy. The United States had only sixteen warships, of which seven were frigates with up to forty-four guns each. In addition, there were some 200 gunboats scattered around the country. Many were unfit for duty and in any event they were small, one-gun boats of no use anywhere except in harbors and inland waters. Great Britain, by contrast, had more than 600 vessels in active service, of which 236 were large ships of the line, or frigates.

The war on land was an almost continuous tale of American defeats, most of them well-earned by inept strategy and poor leadership. Disaster struck first in the northwest. Fort Michilimackinac, in the straits between Lakes Huron and Michigan, surrendered to a British-Canadian and Indian force on July 7, 1812. In mid-August, the small garrison at Fort Dearborn, where later the city of Chicago rose, abandoned the fort on orders. A few miles from the fort the men, women and children were attacked by some 500 Pottawattomie Indians who killed over half the party and captured the rest. Fort Dearborn was named for General Henry Dearborn (1751–1829), who served with distinction in the Revolution and was now in command of the northern frontier from Niagara to the Atlantic. The Dearborn wagon was also named for him. It was a light wagon in which the general rode during one of his campaigns, much to the disgust of his troops who expected a proper general to get about on horseback.

Meanwhile, an American force under General William Hull (1753–1825) was making a bumbling advance into Canada in the Detroit area. Hull soon withdrew to Detroit where, on August 16, he panicked and surrendered without a struggle to an inferior force under the British general, Isaac Brock, who was knighted for his bloodless victory. Hull was convicted of cowardice and sentenced to death at a court-martial two years later. Because of his excellent record in the Revolution, President Madison cancelled the death penalty.

American troops fared no better in the Niagara area. In October a force under Major General Stephen Van Rensselaer (1764–1839) attempted to cross the Niagara River at Queenston and engage a smaller force of the British and their Indian allies. Van Rensselaer, an able and successful man in political life, was an amateur soldier in command of the New York militia. A crossing of the river was effected after considerable difficulty caused by the Americans' own ineptness. The British counterattacked and broke up the American units. Despite Van Rensselaer's urgings, the New York militia refused to cross into Canada to aid their hard-pressed comrades. One American who fought ably at Queenston was Lt. Col. Winfield Scott (1786–1866). He was captured and later exchanged. Scott was wounded in a later battle, was the most important military leader in the Mexican War, ran for president in 1852, and as late as the beginning of the Civil War in 1861 was the general-in-chief of the United States Army. His pompous bearing earned him the nickname of "Old Fuss and Feathers." On the British side, General Brock was killed at Queenston leading an attack on an American position.

Matters took a turn for the better for the United States in early 1813. With naval assistance, troops under Brigadier General Zebulon M. Pike, the discoverer of Pikes Peak, captured York (Toronto) in

April. After the victory, however, an ammunition magazine exploded and killed a number of Americans, including General Pike. The soldiers seized the royal mace from the parliament building and it remained in American hands until 1934 when President Franklin D. Roosevelt had it returned. Late in May, the Americans captured Fort George at the mouth of the Niagara River, and at almost the same time repulsed a British attack on Sackett's Harbor at the eastern end of Lake Ontario.

With a future president of the United States, General William Henry Harrison, now in command in the west, Detroit was recaptured at the end of September. Pursuing the British and Indian forces into Canada, Harrison engaged them in the Battle of the Thames River on October 5, 1813. The result was a substantial victory for the United States. The badly defeated British were commanded by General Henry Procter who fled in disgrace. He was court-martialed and suspended for six months, but later had a distinguished military career. Britain's foremost Indian ally, the Shawnee chief Tecumseh, who for years had been attempting to unite the Indian tribes against the Americans and who, like other Indian leaders, favored the British, was killed in the battle. The Indians fought for the British in the hope that the latter would create an Indian nation in the Northwest Territory if they retook it from the United States. After the Thames defeat and Tecumseh's death, Indian power was measurably weakened and was no longer of much benefit to the British.

The man who is said to have killed Tecumseh was Richard M. Johnson (1781–1850) who was born in a log cabin in Kentucky and was one of the original War Hawks. He resigned from Congress to command a regiment of Kentucky riflemen and was seriously wounded in the Battle of the Thames. Johnson was vice-president during the Van Buren administration, 1837–41. Another American officer who fought with distinction at the Battle of the Thames had special reason for rejoicing at the victory. General Lewis Cass (1782–

1866) had been in command of some of the troops under General Hull and disagreed strongly with the decision to surrender Detroit. Harrison now left Cass in command of Detroit. Cass was governor of Michigan Territory, 1821–31.

The year 1813 did not, however, end auspiciously. In spite of his previous record of treachery, General Wilkinson was named to command the northern border area in the east. He planned an expedition against Montreal, but it was launched too late in the year and was poorly led. After a discouraging defeat at Chrysler's Farm, halfway down the St. Lawrence River to Montreal, Wilkinson called off the campaign in November.

Nor did 1814 look like a good year. In the spring Napoleon was defeated by his enemies and abdicated. This left Great Britain free to use its veteran troops against the United States, and made available more of the ships of the royal navy to seek out American warships and merchantmen. The British overall plan was to tighten the blockade of the East coast and to harass the cities, mount an invasion south along the Lake Champlain route in the north, and to capture New Orleans in the south.

An American army under Brigadier General Jacob Brown (1775–1828) crossed the Niagara, captured Fort Erie and on July 25, engaged the British in the battle of Lundy's Lane, after having won a victory at Chippewa on July 5. Lundy's Lane was one of the hardest-fought battles of the war with heavy casualties on both sides. The American forces afterwards withdrew to Fort Erie. General Brown, who from 1821 to 1828 was the commanding general of the United States Army, was wounded in the engagement.

On the coast, Chesapeake Bay was the center of British activity. A well-trained army, supported by a strong force of warships, landed and advanced on Washington. The military and the government had no plans for the defense of the city and the continuing failure of Madison to appoint strong, capable officials and military leaders became more apparent than ever. Another hapless general, William H. Winder, on August 24, 1814, put his forces in position to meet the enemy near Bladensburg, Maryland, east of the capital. President Madison and most of his cabinet rode out to watch the proceedings, and Secretary of State Monroe gave instructions for placing some troops without consulting General Winder. The British easily routed the Americans. The only Americans who came out of the affair with honor were 400 sailors under Commodore Joshua Barney (1759–1818), who held off ten times that many British troops for half an hour while the regulars and the militia fled. Barney was already a well-known hero for his exploits in the Revolution; he then served in the French navy, and in the War of 1812 was a privateer.

The British advanced on Washington unmolested. They burned most of the city, including the Capitol and the White House. When they reached the White House, they found that President and Mrs. Madison had fled to Virginia so precipitously, that they had left their dinner on the table. British officers ate it. William Thornton, the designer of the Capitol and commissioner of patents since 1802, successfully pleaded with the British not to destroy his office with its models of inventions. When he saw that almost all other officials had abandoned the city, he took charge and prevented plundering. The British stayed in Washington only overnight, and then departed to attack Baltimore. William Hoban, the original designer of the White House, rebuilt it after the war.

On the night of September 13–14, British ships bombarded Fort McHenry, which stood in the path to Baltimore. Watching the bombardment from a British ship where he had gone to try to effect the release of a captured American physician, was a Maryland lawyer, Francis Scott Key (1779–1843). When he saw the flag still flying in the morning, Key was inspired to write "The Star-Spangled Banner" while being returned to shore. The tune was a popular British song, "To Anacreon in Heaven."

The war in the South in 1813 and 1814 was chiefly a matter of Andrew Jackson versus some disaffected Indians. Jackson (1767–1845) was born so near the North Carolina–South Carolina border that both states claim him. When he was thirteen he fought the British in a Revolutionary War skirmish and was captured. Like so many young men of the time, he studied law and then went west to make his fortune. He practiced law in Nashville and speculated in land successfully, becoming a not unusual type of man of the age—a combination of pioneer and aristocrat. In the new state of Tennessee he was a congressman when twenty-nine years old and a senator at thirty. When a man insulted him over a horse race in 1806, Jackson killed him in a duel. Jackson received a bullet near the heart which he carried the rest of his life.

Many Indians still lived in the southern part of the nation, and while most of them did not take sides during the war, some of the Creek Indians were hostile. Their attitude stemmed in part from earlier attempts of Tecumseh to stir them up. A band of Indians attacked Fort Mims, about forty miles north of Mobile, on August 30, 1813, and massacred most of the 550 persons there, including women and children. A volunteer force assembled under the command of Jackson and, heading south, inflicted two defeats on the Indians in November. The following year, on March 27, Jackson with about 2,000 men, including some Cherokee Indian allies, attacked an entrenched Indian force at Horseshoe Bend in Mississippi Territory. The Indians were almost annihilated, 350 bodies being counted within their fortification. Jackson was promoted to major general and in August he forced the Indians to sign a treaty by which the Creeks gave up a fifth of Georgia and three-fifths of what became Alabama. Finally, in November, Jackson made an unauthorized foray into Spanish Florida, capturing Pensacola and ending a British threat from that direction.

Meanwhile, a large force of British troops, protected by a for-

midable fleet, descended on the Gulf of Mexico to attack New Orleans. Jackson was given command of the American forces and
gathered a mixed army of regulars, militiamen, Blacks and Choctaw
Indians. Selecting a strong position between the Mississippi River
and a swamp, Jackson fortified it with earthworks and artillery. On
the morning of January 8, 1815, more than 5,000 British troops under
the command of General Sir Edward Pakenham, a distinguished
veteran of the Napoleonic wars, attacked the American positions
head on. The result was a defeat and a slaughter in which the British
lost 2,000 men killed, wounded and missing. Among the dead was
General Pakenham. The American losses were only eight killed and
thirteen wounded. The British withdrew to their ships and sailed
away. None of those engaged knew it at the time, but the Battle of
New Orleans was fought two weeks after a treaty of peace ending the
war had been signed in Ghent. Among Jackson's army was a band
of pirates and smugglers under their leader Jean Lafitte (1782–1854).
Lafitte had refused a British offer of £30,000 and an officer's commission and had joined the Americans in the battle. President Madison later pardoned Lafitte and his crew in return for their aid.

Americans fared much better at sea than on land in the War of
1812, although the victories won on the ocean were one-to-one sea
battles which were excellent for morale but had no effect on the out-
come of the war. Victories in two naval engagements on inland waters
were more significant and possibly prevented more disastrous events
on land than took place. From the beginning, though, the British
navy ruled the seas. At first Britain left American merchant shipping
almost untouched. The British thought the fact they had rescinded
their orders against neutral shipping would bring an early peace in
spite of the formal declaration of war. The British also needed the
supplies being carried in American ships. Late in 1812 a blockade of
the exits from Delaware Bay and Chesapeake Bay was established.
The blockade was extended in May, 1813, from Long Island to the

Mississippi. It was a year more, though, before the New England coast was formally put under blockade. Until then the British desisted in order to encourage anti-war feeling, which was strongest in New England.

Some of the notable single ship fights involved the *Constitution, United States, Essex* and *Chesapeake.* The *Constitution,* commanded by Captain Isaac Hull (1773–1843), who had been at sea since he was fourteen and was a nephew of the ill-fated General Hull, met H.M.S. *Guerrière* about 750 miles east of Boston on August 19, 1812. The *Constitution* was somewhat larger but it was Hull's seamanship and the fury of the broadsides from American cannons that so crippled the *Guerrière* that its captain had to surrender. News of this first sea victory reached the East coast a few days before the bad news of General Hull's inexcusable surrender at Detroit. While the latter was more serious, the sea victory was more spectacular and did much to keep up the nation's morale. Lamenting that "never before in the history of the world did an English frigate strike to an American," the *Times* of London said this would make the Americans "insolent and confident."

Late in the year, the *Constitution,* now under the command of Captain William Bainbridge (1774–1833), added to the career that was making it the most famous ship in American naval history by destroying the *Java* off the coast of Brazil. Another of America's largest frigates, the *United States,* engaged the British ship *Macedonia* west of the Canary Islands on October 25. The *Macedonia* was faster but the *United States* was more heavily armed. Exploiting mistakes in seamanship by the British, the American commander, Captain Stephen Decatur (1779–1820), had the *Macedonia* beaten before it got within 100 yards of his ship.

Captain David Porter (1780–1843), in command of the *Essex,* was ordered to join other American warships in the South Atlantic in late 1812, but when he missed them he decided to go around Cape

Horn into the Pacific. This he did, the first ship of the United States Navy to sail that ocean. He found so many unguarded British merchant ships there that he could hardly take care of them all after they were captured. His foster son, David Glasgow Farragut (1801–70), was with him as a midshipman, and was put in charge of one prize ship even though he was only thirteen years old. Farragut became an admiral and the leading naval hero of the North in the Civil War. British warships finally caught up with the *Essex* at Valparaiso, Chile, in February, 1814. Foster was blockaded in the harbor for over a month, and when he tried to escape the superior British force battered his ship to pieces, causing heavy American casualties.

The frigate *Chesapeake,* the victim in the 1807 affair with the *Leopard,* continued to have bad luck. Under the command of Captain James Lawrence (1781–1813) it met H.M.S. *Shannon* off the Massachusetts coast on June 1, 1813. Superior gunnery on the part of the British made a wreck of the *Chesapeake* and Lawrence was mortally wounded. It was then, as he was being carried below, that he is reported to have said, "Don't give up the ship." No member of his crew hauled down the flag but the British, in hand-to-hand fighting, swarmed aboard and took possession.

One of the few crucial battles of the war was fought near the western end of Lake Erie on September 10, 1813. With nine ships, most of them hurriedly built on the lake, Captain Oliver Hazard Perry (1785–1819) met a somewhat weaker British flotilla of six similar ships. Perry was so short of sailors to man his ships that he hastily made seamen out of a hundred men of the Kentucky militia. They gave a good account of themselves. The battle was fiercely and closely fought. Perry's flagship, the *Lawrence,* was so badly damaged that he had himself rowed to the *Niagara,* where he resumed the battle. He took with him his banner—which had inscribed on it the recent words of the unfortunate Captain Lawrence—and his brother, Matthew Calbraith Perry (1794–1858), who forty years later opened

Japan to the western world. After several hours of hard fighting, the British surrendered. The victory gave the United States control of Lake Erie and opened the way for General Harrison to retake Detroit and advance into Canada. To Harrison, Perry dispatched his famous message: "We have met the enemy and they are ours." Six years later, on a diplomatic mission to Venezuela, Perry died of yellow fever in Trinidad.

An equally significant naval battle occurred just a year and a day later, on September 11, 1814, on Lake Champlain, between New York and Vermont. During the summer the British prepared for an invasion southward into the United States by the Lake Champlain route. The land forces available were veterans of the Duke of Wellington's campaigns against Napoleon, and a fleet was gathered on the lake. American land forces fortified Plattsburg, on the New York side, and a small fleet was organized there. Its four warships and ten gunboats were under the command of Captain Thomas MacDonough (1783–1825). The British fleet sailed down the lake to attack Mac-Donough while the British army, under the command of General Sir George Prevost, approached Plattsburg. In a joint land and water action, the British troops were repulsed while the British fleet, roughly equal in numbers and power to the Americans, was badly defeated and withdrew such of its ships as remained navigable. General Prevost lost heart, dared not advance south with the Americans in command of the lake, and retreated to Canada.

Privateering, the practice of privately owned, armed ships preying on the commerce of the enemy, was encouraged by both sides in the War of 1812. More than 500 American ships registered as privateers, but most of them were small and many made only one cruise. The privateers captured about 1,300 British ships with cargoes worth millions of dollars. Otway Burns (c. 1775–1850) outfitted a Baltimore clipper, the *Snap-Dragon,* and caused so much havoc to enemy shipping that the British put a price of $50,000 on his head. Another

American owner sent out the *True-Blooded Yankee* in March, 1813. Cruising along the coasts of Ireland and Scotland, this ship in thirty-seven days took twenty-seven vessels as prizes. It also captured a town in Scotland and burned seven ships in the harbor. The *Chausseur*, sailing near Cuba in February, 1814, mistook a British royal navy schooner for a merchant ship. Realizing this too late, the *Chausseur's* commander gave fight and in ten minutes forced the British ship to surrender. The American captain reported to the ship's owners: "When I found myself deceived, the honor of the flag intrusted to my care was not to be disgraced by flight." The British were not idle and privateers from the British Isles and Canada captured a good many American merchantmen. One privateer, the *Liver-Pool Packet,* counted at least forty-four ships as its victims.

Diplomatic moves to end the war had been underway almost from the time it started. The Russian czar Alexander I offered to mediate, but the British refused the offer. Direct negotiations between representatives of the two sides began in Ghent, Belgium, in August, 1814. At first the British made large demands. These included the setting up of an Indian state under British influence in the area north of the Ohio River, and access to the northern part of the Mississippi River. The Americans refused to consider such proposals. The attitudes of the two sides changed from time to time, depending on the latest news from the battlefronts. When word of the American victory at Plattsburg reached Ghent in October, the British became more amenable to a settlement. On Christmas Eve the American delegation—which included Albert Gallatin, Henry Clay and John Quincy Adams, son of former president Adams—and the British signed a treaty. The Senate ratified it in February, 1815. About all the treaty did was to end the fighting. Not a word was said about impressment or the rights of neutral commerce, the reasons for which presumably the United States had originally gone to war.

The war and its end did have some indirect and beneficial results. A commercial treaty with Great Britain was negotiated in 1815, and agreement was reached on how to settle peacefully any boundary disputes that might arise between the United States and Canada. Britain from now on recognized that the United States was a truly independent nation and must be treated as such. America, on the other hand, realized that Canada was British and was going to stay that way. The fact that American forces had at least fought the British to a standstill increased national pride in spite of the widespread opposition to the war. The end of the fighting and the arrival of a long peace in Europe in 1815 meant that the nation could turn its attention away from foreign affairs and direct its energies toward internal problems and opportunities, such as the expansion of the frontier and of American industry.

While the war was coming to a close, the feeling against it in New England grew so strong that one faction there was on the verge of urging secession from the union. Extreme Federalists wanted New England to propose certain changes in the Constitution; if they were not accepted, New England would go its own way. Others were more moderate but believed that New England was in danger of being ruined by the war and the policies of the Federal government. At the call of Massachusetts, twenty-six men gathered at Hartford, Connecticut, on December 15, 1814, representing chiefly Massachusetts, Rhode Island and Connecticut. As the historian Henry Adams wrote of them later, the delegates were "mostly cautious and elderly men, who detested democracy, but disliked enthusiasm almost as much." As it turned out, the moderate Federalists were in control and secession was not seriously considered. The sessions were secret but when the convention adjourned on January 5, 1815, it issued a public report. The report attacked President Madison, but otherwise discussed New England's grievances in rather vague terms. When, shortly thereafter, news both of Jackson's victory at New Orleans and of the peace treaty reached the East, the men of the Hartford Convention, and through them the Federalists in general, were put in the position of being unpatriotic defeatists. The Federalist party never recovered from this blow.

Hardly had one war ended when another began. On March 2, 1815, Congress declared war on Algiers, making official the armed conflict between the United States and the Barbary States of North Africa that had been going on much of the time since 1801. These states, Algiers, Tunis, Morocco and Tripoli, had preyed on merchant shipping as pirates since the sixteenth century. For the most part, the European nations found it more practical to pay tribute to the pirates to let their ships alone than to fight them. The new United States adopted this policy and by 1800 had paid about $2,000,000 in tribute. The situation changed in 1801 when the Pasha of Tripoli, seeking a larger annual tribute from the United States, declared war by having the American flag at the consulate torn down. Jefferson, as peaceful as he was, would stand such indignities no longer and dispatched some American naval vessels to the Mediterranean. An off-and-on, undeclared war went on until 1805 when Tripoli gave up and promised not to prey on American ships any more.

As time passed, however, the North African pirates took up their favorite activity again. The Napoleonic wars, with the European powers locked in a struggle among themselves, gave the Barbary pirates an opportunity to attack shipping without much chance of retaliation. Captain Stephen Decatur was dispatched with a force of ten vessels in May, 1815. He captured two Algerian ships and made his way into the harbor at Algiers on June 30. Decatur forced the ruler, the Dey, to sign a treaty whereby he agreed to desist from further piratical acts, and to free any American prisoners he held without payment of ransom. The other pirate strongholds soon accepted similar terms and never troubled the United States again.

Decatur came home to a hero's welcome, and on one public occasion offered the toast for which he is remembered: "Our country!

In her intercourse with foreign nations, may she always be in the right; but our country, right or wrong." Other American naval officers who acquired some of the skill they later demonstrated in the War of 1812 while fighting the Barbary pirates included Isaac Hull, David Porter, Thomas MacDonough and William Bainbridge. The group also included the unfortunate James Barron (1769–1851) who had command of the *Chesapeake* when that ship was halted and fired on in 1807 by a British warship in search of deserters. Barron was found guilty by a court-martial in 1808 of not having his ship ready for action and was suspended for five years. Some years later, convinced that Decatur as a member of the Board of Navy Commissioners was preventing his return to full honorable standing in the navy, Barron challenged Decatur to a duel and shot him dead. Barron was reinstated in the navy in 1821 but his career remained under a cloud.

By the end of the Algerian War, Madison was more than half-way through his second term. In six years in office, the unwarlike Virginian had spent most of his time dealing with controversies with foreign nations and fighting an unpopular war.

5 Monroe and His Doctrine

THE CAMPAIGN for the presidency in 1816 disclosed even less organized opposition to the Republicans than before. James Monroe of
Virginia, like his predecessor, moved up from the position of secretary of state. Monroe's running mate was Daniel D. Tompkins (1774–
1825), who had been governor of New York since 1807. Rufus King
was the Federalist candidate for president, but the party hardly existed in most states. King carried Massachusetts, Connecticut and
Delaware, and Monroe won in the Electoral College vote, 138 to 34.

James Monroe (1758–1831), Virginia born as were Jefferson and
Madison, left William and Mary College at the age of eighteen to
join the Revolutionary Army and was wounded at the Battle of Trenton. After the war he studied law under Jefferson and their lifelong
friendship began at that time. Monroe was not at the Constitutional
Convention and, in fact, opposed ratification because he thought it
made the central government too strong. Nevertheless, he became a
United States senator in 1790, and from then on his life was one of
public service in which he held almost every kind of position. He
was governor of Virginia and minister or special envoy to France and
other countries, and was one of the Americans who negotiated the
Louisiana Purchase. Secretary of state during most of Madison's two
terms, he also acted as secretary of war in the latter part of the War
of 1812. On taking office as president, he selected able men for the

chief cabinet posts: John Quincy Adams of Massachusetts for the State Department, John C. Calhoun for the War Department and William H. Crawford (1772–1834), a fellow Virginian, for the Treasury Department. Crawford had been a senator, minister to France and secretary of war under Madison.

Monroe was a tall man, dignified but unpretentious, who liked public service for its own sake rather than for personal prestige. During the year in which he took office, Monroe made a three-and-a-half months' tour of the country, going as far west as Detroit. He received a warm welcome everywhere, even from Federalist New England. His personality and his obvious intention to be moderate in his actions and policies won him general approval. Mrs. Monroe, who as a young woman had been an active participant in the social life of New York City, was a beautiful and regally gracious hostess in the White House, but chronic illness kept her from making as much of a social mark as had her predecessor, Dolley Madison. The Monroe's youngest daughter, Maria, became the first daughter of a president to be married in the White House, in March, 1820.

Because of the absence of formal party politics and the optimistic attitude of the nation as a whole, the period of Monroe's two terms in the presidency came to be known as "The Era of Good Feelings." In a general way this was true enough, but disputes and problems were shaping up in several areas. The division of opinion between advocates of a strong federal government and those supporting states' rights continued to exist and was brought out in the debates over protective tariffs and internal improvements. When these matters were argued, differences also appeared between North and South, agricultural and industrial interests, the frontier West and the increasingly urban East. Slavery stirred up conflict between its opponents and its proponents. Sectional and economic interests thus became more important than constitutional theory.

Out of the needs and desires of the nation in its mood of optimistic nationalism came the "American System," although the phrase as such was not used until March, 1824, when Henry Clay included it in a speech on the tariff. By any name, the American System claimed to bring together the business and industrial interests of the East and the farming and pioneering interests of the West. The American System was based on two programs: a protective tariff and internal improvements (that is, public works at federal government expense). The prewar embargo and the war itself cut the United States off from its usual sources of manufactured goods, chiefly Great Britain. This in turn, as noted, encouraged some American businessmen to start manufacturing operations of their own. The moment the war ended, however, British goods flowed into the country at marked-down prices in order to dispose of accumulated surpluses. This hurt, and in some cases ruined, the newly established American firms. A cry went up for a protective tariff to keep British products from underselling domestic goods.

This program was also favored by nationalistic elements—the War Hawks and men of similar mind. They proposed to link a protective tariff to internal improvements, the latter meaning chiefly roads and canals to aid farmers in getting their food and other raw materials to market. The nationalists' theory was that the combination of the two would expand the domestic market for manufactured goods by increasing the prosperity of farmers and workers, encourage American manufacturers to produce more and cheaper goods, and, finally, make the United States less dependent on foreign products.

Henry Clay and John C. Calhoun were two of the leading spokesmen for the American System. They headed a faction of the Republican party which advocated policies of much the same nature as those favored by the Federalists. They believed the central government had wide power and should use it in the national interest. Their actions hastened the break within the party between these new nationalists and those who held to the Jeffersonian belief in states' rights and a comparatively weak federal government. Calhoun summed up the argument for federal action in 1817:

> We are greatly and rapidly—I was about to say fearfully—growing. This is our pride and our danger; our weakness and our strength. . . . Let us, then, bind the Republic together with a perfect system of roads and canals.

In addition, a protective tariff, he declared, "would make the parts adhere more closely. . . . It would form a new and most powerful cement." In short, Calhoun was saying, the United States was a powerful nation and it needed to be thought of as one unit, not as a group of associated states.

The first step toward activating the American System was taken as far back as 1806. At that time Congress voted to begin building a National Road from east to west. It was to start at Cumberland, Maryland, and for that reason the first part of it was familiarly known as the Cumberland Road. President Jefferson had to face the constitutional problem of whether the Federal government could plan, build and pay for public works, such as this road that would run through several different states. The Jeffersonian school of thought was practical enough to want to do such things, but believed that an amendment to the Constitution was necessary.

In his last message to Congress in December, 1816, Madison took the same position. He, in fact, recommended a Federal program of road and canal construction, but made it clear he believed the Constitution would have to be amended first. That same month Calhoun introduced a bill to create a permanent fund for such improvements, using money that would be paid to the government by the Bank of the United States. The bill passed, although the vote showed how the different sections felt about such measures: the West was all for it; New England and the middle states were against it because, while they favored a protective tariff, they did not want to pay for western roads; the South was almost evenly divided, still uncertain where its economic interest lay. Madison, in his last official act as president, vetoed the bill as contrary to the Constitution.

President Monroe held the same view. When Congress passed a bill in 1822 to repair the National Road and set up toll gates on it, he vetoed it on the grounds that a constitutional amendment was needed. Monroe later relented, to the extent that he signed a bill in 1824 under which the government would undertake a survey of the nation's needs for military, commercial and postal roads and canals. The next year he approved a subscription by the Federal government of $300,000 to the Chesapeake and Delaware Canal Company.

By the end of Monroe's second administration, two opposing movements were discernible. On the one hand, fewer people were inclined to argue against the right of the government in Washington to undertake internal improvements; on the other hand, economic and geographical interests led some people to favor or oppose specific measures on the basis of what would seem to be to their advantage. In the South, for instance, opposition to protective tariffs mounted as it became clear that the region was to become primarily a raw-materials producer—chiefly cotton—and an importer of manufactured goods from abroad or from the North. The influences of geography as well as economics also determined that the most important roads and canals would tie the West to the North, not to the South. This change in the thought of a whole region can be traced plainly in the career of Calhoun. Starting out as a leader of the War Hawks, a nationalist and an advocate of internal improvements, this South Carolinian later became the symbol of southern interests and the most eloquent advocate of states' rights.

In foreign affairs during Monroe's first term, two events did much to consolidate the peace and security of the United States. The less spectacular of the two was the Rush-Bagot Convention, effective in 1818. By this agreement between the United States and Great

Britain, a number of problems left over from the War of 1812 were resolved amicably. The boundary between the United States and Canada was settled as running along the 49th parallel from Lake of Woods to the crest of the Rocky Mountains, thus, in effect, accepting the rather vague northern boundary of the Louisiana Purchase. It was agreed that the rest of the land west, the Oregon Territory, would be open for ten years to joint occupation. Presumably the two nations would then extend the agreement or make a new arrangement. The convention also gave fishing privileges off the shores of Labrador and Newfoundland to the United States. These rights had been sought for many years.

Perhaps the most important item in the agreement was the provision for almost total disarmament along the American–Canadian border, including the removal of warships from the Great Lakes. The convention was named for Charles Bagot, the British minister in Washington, and Richard Rush (1780–1859), who was acting temporarily as secretary of state. Rush, a native of Pennsylvania and son of the noted physician and signer of the Declaration of Independence, Benjamin Rush, had already been attorney general. A decade later, Rush spent two years in Britain negotiating the details of the bequest to the United States of James Smithson, an Englishman, that resulted in the establishment of the Smithsonian Institution.

The events leading to the acquisition of Florida were more spectacular than the agreement concerning America's northern boundary. From Jefferson's time on, many Americans wanted to acquire Florida. In an era when colonies changed hands overnight through treaties— some of which might be secret—the United States had considerable interest in who ruled Florida; a weak power such as Spain, or a strong one that might be a threat, such as Great Britain or France. Inhabitants of the South and Southwest had their eyes on Florida as logical territory for the expansion of southern agriculture and slavery. They, and the rest of the nation, were irritated by border raids carried out occasionally by Indians, including at times escaped slaves as well.

When the United States acquired Louisiana, there were two Floridas. West Florida, a piece of land extending from the Mississippi eastward to the Perdido River, was claimed as part of the Louisiana Purchase, but Spain disputed the claim. Under Madison, the United States occupied part of this area, to the Pearl River, and declared it part of Louisiana. Two years later, the boundary was advanced eastward to the Perdido River, again by unilateral American action. The Perdido became the western boundary of the present state of Florida, while the territory between the Pearl and Perdido rivers ended up as parts of Alabama and Mississippi.

So matters stood through the War of 1812. After the war, East Florida, which was all of Florida east of the Perdido, continued to be a refuge for hostile Indians who threatened the Georgia border. After a few forays into Florida by American forces to put down the threat, General Andrew Jackson in late 1817 was given charge of the problem. In his usual no-nonsense manner, he marched his forces into Florida and not only attacked Indians but also, in April and May, 1818, seized two Spanish towns. In the course of pursuing the Indians, Jackson captured Alexander Arbuthnot, a Scots trader whom he accused of having warned the Indians he was coming, and Robert Ambrister, an English trader who, he charged, had stirred up the Indians against the Americans. Jackson court-martialed them both and had Arbuthnot hanged and Ambrister shot. Newspapers in England denounced Jackson as a "ruffian," but the British government decided to ignore the affair. Some congressmen censured Jackson for his actions, but the public generally approved.

The posts seized from the Spaniards were returned to them, but the Spanish government, weak at home and facing revolt in its Latin American colonies, could see that all Florida would have to be handed over to the United States. The Adams-Onís Treaty of 1819,

named for the American secretary of state and the Spanish minister
in Washington, ceded Florida to the United States. In return, the
latter renounced claims to Texas which had been put forward at the
time of the Louisiana Purchase, and also assumed debts owed to
Americans by Spain, up to $5,000,000. The treaty also defined the
hitherto uncertain boundary of the Louisiana Purchase. The boundary line was to run from the mouth of the Sabine River on the Gulf
of Mexico northwestward to the 42nd parallel. From there the boundary line was to continue due west to the Pacific Ocean, which meant
that Spain was giving up any claims to the Pacific Northwest.

On the domestic scene and in the area of judicial powers, the
Supreme Court continued to set precedents that increased the powers of the judiciary and the national government, while also buttress-
ing property rights. The case of *McCulloch* vs. *Maryland* in 1819
gave Chief Justice Marshall an opportunity to assert the power of the
Federal government over the states. Maryland had levied a tax on a
branch of the Bank of the United States in Baltimore. In his opinion
Marshall strengthened the "implied powers" conferred on the government in the Constitution. He argued that if the government had
the right to coin money, as stated, it was implied that it could establish a bank. If that were so, then the government was supreme in that
sphere and a state, as an inferior body, could not tax an instrument
of the superior government. This is generally agreed to be Marshall's
most brilliant opinion on constitutional law, but it was by no means
universally accepted at the time.

The same year, in the Dartmouth College Case, the court rendered a decision that aided the judicial protection of property rights.
The State of New Hampshire, without the consent of Dartmouth
College, amended the college's charter which, in legal terms, was a
contract. As was so often the case, Marshall himself wrote the court's
decision. In it he ruled New Hampshire's act was unconstitutional
because it violated Article I, Section 10, of the Constitution which

prohibited any state from passing any law "impairing the Obligation of Contracts."

As lawyer for Dartmouth, Daniel Webster (1782–1852) added to his growing reputation as an orator and debater. A native of New Hampshire, Webster was in the House of Representatives during most of the War of 1812. He was much opposed to it but he did not take part in the Hartford Convention. During the course of the court case, Webster, a Dartmouth graduate, remarked: "It is, sir, as I have said, a small college, and yet there are those who love it." More typical of his style, and of the approved style of public orators of the time, were his remarks at the laying of the cornerstone for the Bunker Hill Monument in June, 1825, on the occasion of the fiftieth anniversary of the battle there:

> We wish that this column, rising towards heaven among the pointed spires of so many temples dedicated to God, may contribute also to produce in all minds a pious feeling of dependence and gratitude. We wish, finally, that the last object to the sight of him who leaves his native shore, and the first to gladden his who revisits it, may be something which shall remind him of the liberty and glory of his country.

The power of the Federal government was bolstered in the area of regulation of interstate commerce in 1824 when the Supreme Court, in another decision written by Marshall, ruled that Congress had sole power and that states had no authority over commerce between two or more states. This case, *Gibbons* vs. *Ogden,* involved a monopoly granted by New York State to operate steamboats. When an unauthorized rival began operating a line between New York and New Jersey, he was sued but was successful in an appeal to the Supreme Court, which ruled that New York had no right to grant such a monopoly.

The first serious clash between slavery and antislavery interests, in 1819–20, strained relations between North and South, produced a long and tense legislative battle in Congress, and hinted menacingly at worse trouble to come. At the close of 1819 the union consisted of eleven free and eleven slave states. The North was outdistancing the South in population, and so held a numerical advantage in the House of Representatives. Southern leaders felt strongly, therefore, that the number of slave and free states must remain balanced so that the South would at least have as many votes in the Senate as the North.

Maine, until now a part of Massachusetts and certain to be free territory, and Missouri, part of the Louisiana Purchase, were ready for statehood. The first assumption was that they would be admitted one free, one slave, to maintain the precarious balance of power. When Congress considered the necessary legislation, however, a northern representative introduced an amendment that would pro- hibit bringing any more slaves into Missouri, and would set free all children born of slaves there when they reached the age of twenty- five. After much maneuvering and debating, running on into March, 1820, a final compromise was reached. Maine was admitted as a free state and Missouri as a slave state, but slavery was forever prohibited in the rest of the Louisiana Purchase north of the line of latitude 36 degrees, 30 minutes. This was the southern boundary of Missouri, so the Arkansas and Oklahoma areas remained open to slavery but not the great extent of land to the north and west.

This Missouri Compromise, with Henry Clay as one of its chief negotiators, put off a further showdown on the issue of the expansion of slave territory for thirty years. At the same time, though, it em- phasized the widening division over slavery. The South believed that slave labor was vital to the production of its staple crop, cotton. The slaves in the nation by now were worth at least $300,000,000. Thus circumstances forced southern leaders to defend the institution and to fight for its extension. In retirement at Monticello, Thomas Jeffer- son rightly said when he heard the news of the Missouri Compromise that it was "a fire bell in the night."

The year of the Missouri Compromise brought also the nation's ninth presidential election. No formal nomination or campaign was necessary as no one cared to challenge Monroe. In the Electoral College he received all but one vote. An elector in New Hampshire cast his vote for John Quincy Adams. He claimed he did so because he thought no one after Washington should have the honor of being elected president unanimously, but it was known that the elector did not like Monroe personally.

In his second term Monroe's attention in foreign affairs focused on Latin America and its relations with Europe and the United States. As late as 1810, practically all of Latin America was the colonial preserve of Spain and Portugal. Many Latin Americans did not at this time desire independence, although they were agitating for more equality with the home governments. When Napoleon deposed the Spanish and Portuguese monarchs, the colonies were cut off from the homeland and had to fend for themselves. In addition, both the American and the French revolutions influenced some Latin American leaders to favor taking similar action.

The United States kept an interested eye on developments to the south, partly because of natural sympathy for colonies seeking independence, partly for more practical reasons. The disruption of trade with Europe during the Napoleonic era and the War of 1812 encouraged shippers and merchants to seek other trade outlets. As early as 1810 President Madison sent Joel Roberts Poinsett (1779–1851) of South Carolina to study at first hand the situation of the countries in Latin America and what they were doing about independence. Poinsett was gone four years. Besides information, he brought back a flowering plant which was named after him—the poinsettia. President Monroe, beginning to face the problem of whether to recognize the independence of Latin American lands, decided in May, 1817, to send three commissioners southward to observe the situation. The men, however, did not set sail until December.

Henry Clay in Congress and Secretary of State Adams were at odds as to whether the United States should recognize promptly the independence of Latin American nations. The disagreement stemmed partly from the fact that Clay and Adams were likely rivals for the presidency in 1824, but it was also the result of their different appraisals of the situation. Clay demanded in March, 1818, that diplomatic recognition be granted the new nations. He believed they would be like the United States and would join with the states in forming a neutral bloc against European intrigues. So far as sentiment ruled, many Americans sided with Clay in wanting to acknowledge fellow fighters for independence. While most of the new nations abolished slavery, they were seldom democratic and were often under the rule of military dictatorships.

Adams took a less sentimental view of the question. He did not doubt that the various colonies would become independent, and he defended the right of the United States to recognize that fact if it wished. He saw no need to rush, however. Nor did he think the Latin lands were going to be much like the United States in character, nor would they offer any worthwhile commercial advantages.

Events were moving forward in Latin America in the meantime. Paraguay was independent as early as 1811 under a local dictator. Between then and 1828, the other nations won their independence. Two men in particular emerged as symbols of the struggle, and as the leaders in a good deal of the whole continent: Simón Bolívar (1783–1830) and José de San Martín (1788–1850). Bolívar, born in Caracas of a wealthy family, became for a while the most powerful man on the South American continent. The armed forces he led defeated the Spaniards and he became the first president of Gran Colombia, which had formerly been the Spanish viceroyalty of New Granada. Within a decade Gran Colombia broke up into four separate nations: Venezuela, Colombia, Ecuador and Panama. San Martín, born in Argentina, was the leader responsible for freeing Argentina and Chile from Spanish rule, while he and Bolívar, in their one meeting of forces, both helped Peru achieve independence.

Brazil, the only Portuguese colony, had a different experience. Following Napoleon's invasion of Portugal, the ruler, King John VI, fled to Brazil, so that for some years Rio de Janeiro was the capital city of the Portuguese empire. When John VI returned to Lisbon in 1821, he left his son behind as regent. The people of Brazil wanted independence and in September, 1822, the son proclaimed himself Pedro I, emperor of Brazil, under a constitutional monarchy.

By early March, 1822, Monroe felt the time for action had come and he recommended to Congress that the United States extend recognition to its neighbors to the south. Congress agreed, appropriated money for sending diplomats to Latin America, and in May Monroe formally recognized the independence of Argentina, Chile, Colombia, Mexico and Peru.

The danger remained that Spain, aided by other European nations, might try to reconquer its colonies. At one point it seemed that France, now ruled by a restored Bourbon monarchy with Louis XVIII as king, would help Spain in this endeavor. France was encouraged by the other members of the Holy Alliance, the czar of Russia, the emperor of Austria and the king of Prussia. Great Britain reacted strongly against any possible intervention of this kind, partly to prevent an increase in the power of the continental nations, partly because she had come out of the Napoleonic wars with a profitable advantage in trade with Latin America. The British foreign minister, George Canning, proposed in August, 1823, that the United States join Britain in warning France not to help Spain in the New World. Monroe consulted his two predecessors, Jefferson and Madison, and although they had once been enemies of Great Britain, they advised accepting Canning's suggestion. Secretary of State Adams, however, did not think the United States should join Britain. He was skeptical of British motives and thought that Britain, as the stronger power, would dominate any joint Anglo-American move.

Monroe accepted Adams's view, but did not agree with him that the policy statement on Latin America should be in the form of communications directly to the various governments. In the end, with Adams doing most of the actual drafting, what became the Monroe Doctrine was made a part of Monroe's annual message to Congress on December 2, 1823. He said:

> In the wars of the European powers in matters relating to themselves we have never taken any part, nor does it comport with our policy to do so. It is only when our rights are invaded or seriously menaced that we resent injuries or make preparation for our defense. . . .
>
> We owe, therefore, to candor and to the amicable relations existing between the United States and those powers to declare that we should consider any attempt on their part to extend their system to any portion of this hemisphere as dangerous to our peace and safety. With the existing colonies or dependencies of any European power we have not interfered and shall not interfere. But with the Governments who have declared their independence and maintained it, and whose independence we have, on great consideration and on just principles, acknowledged, we could not view any interposition for the purpose of oppressing them, or controlling in any other manner their destiny, by any European power in any other light than as the manifestation of an unfriendly disposition toward the United States.

In a word, Europe should stay out of the Western Hemisphere hereafter and not interfere with any independent nation. The message was in part directed also at Russia because Alexander I claimed Russian ownership of the northwestern part of the North American continent as far south as the 51st latitude, an area lying within Oregon Territory. Russia also forbade foreign shipping to enter the waters around the territory Russia claimed. After long negotiations, Russia backed down and in April, 1824, accepted a boundary farther north, at 54 degrees, 40 minutes latitude. Great Britain officially agreed with the American view on the Western Hemisphere, but cast some doubt on American motives. The despotic continental powers pretended not to take the Monroe message seriously and considered the United States "haughty" and "arrogant." Nevertheless, the message was effective to the extent that no foreign nation chose seriously to challenge it.

By the time of the presidential election of 1824, it was plain that one era of party politics was ending. The Republicans were the only party, but divided into so many factions, backing different candidates with contrasting views on public issues, that no fewer than five men first entered the contest: John Quincy Adams, John C. Calhoun, Henry Clay, William H. Crawford and Andrew Jackson. A stroke damaged Crawford's candidacy, while Calhoun withdrew to run for vice-president with Jackson. Jackson received the most popular votes and also the most electoral votes, ninety-nine. He did not have a majority, however, for Adams received eighty-four; Crawford, forty-one; Clay, thirty-seven. For the second time in twenty-four years the decision was thrown into the House of Representatives. The House had to choose from among the top three, and so Clay was eliminated. He threw his influence to Adams and in February Adams was elected president, thirteen states, the minimum number, voting for him, seven for Jackson and four for Crawford. Some Jackson followers charged that Clay and Adams had made a "corrupt bargain" whereby Adams would appoint Clay secretary of state. No evidence to this effect was ever presented, even though the appointment was made. The election of Adams meant that of the first six presidents of the nation, four were Virginians and two were from Massachusetts, the latter two being father and son. The election was also the last for the Republican party. It divided into two parties, the Adams-Clay faction becoming the National Republicans (later the Whig party) and the Jackson followers the Democratic Republicans (later the Democratic party).

John Quincy Adams (1767–1848), of Puritan descent, was short and stout, with a grim mouth, and tended to be a careless dresser. Reserved in manner, sometimes seeming harsh, he was a man of principle. He also had the courage to act on his principles which sometimes made him unpopular as a political figure. Adams did not get along well with people. On the other hand, he was an excellent secretary of state and a devoted public servant. As a young man he accompanied his father on some of the latter's diplomatic missions abroad. Later he served as a diplomat himself and in 1803 was elected a senator. Although nominally a Federalist at that time, he supported Jefferson on such matters as the Louisiana Purchase and the Embargo Act. His succession to the presidency from the department of state (the same path followed by Madison and Monroe) was logical and deserved, but he was destined for an unhappy administration and defeat when he sought a second term.

The election of Adams also ended the Virginia Dynasty which had held the chief executive's office for twenty-four years, and, on the whole, successfully and to the nation's advantage. When Monroe, the last of them, departed, the nation had grown to twenty-four states. Besides Maine and Missouri, five other states were admitted in the Madison and Monroe regimes: Louisiana, 1812; Indiana, 1816; Mississippi, 1817; Illinois, 1818; and Alabama, 1819.

6 Business—Industry—Labor—Agriculture

BETWEEN 1800 AND 1825, the American economy grew, changed and enjoyed general prosperity except for one depression. The country continued to be chiefly agricultural, but slightly less so proportionately than at the beginning of the quarter century. Shipping remained an enterprise at which Americans did well, but it, too, held a smaller share of the total economic enterprise. Manufacturing, of very little importance in 1800, was a significant part of the national economy twenty-five years later.

The West grew faster than any other section and became a major source of agricultural products. The new manufacturing plants sprang up mostly in the North and East, while the South settled more firmly into a cotton-growing economy based on slave labor. Of those gainfully employed in 1820, about 72 per cent were in agriculture; 12 per cent in manufacturing and mechanical work; 10 per cent in domestic and other personal service; and 3 per cent in the professions.

The dominant figure in business at the start of the century was the merchant capitalist. Such men were often shipowners, exporters, wholesalers, bankers and insurers. From them came the capital to build the early factories and machinery. Labor to run machinery was comparatively scarce and expensive. Industrial machinery itself was more complicated and was used more widely. As a result, the division of labor, whereby a man performed only one or a few steps in the manufacturing process, became more commonly practiced. Machinery at first was powered by hand or by horses. Waterpower was the next source of power to be developed and this meant, of course, that plants had to be located on rivers. Steam power appears to have had its first use for running factory machinery at a New York State sawmill in 1803.

The early manufacturing companies were usually partnerships or joint-stock companies, which amounted to enlarged partnerships. The corporation did not become popular until general laws made it easy to form. New York State passed the first general incorporation law in 1811.

The textile industry was America's first manufacturing enterprise of consequence, although it had to compete with the British textile manufacturers. While cotton was easily available from the South, and New England had excellent waterpower sites, the machinery had to be copied from the British who invented it. In 1800 about 2,000 spindles were in operation; by 1810 the number rose to 80,000; and five years later, spurred by the wartime cutoff of British goods, to 500,000 spindles.

Moses Brown (1738–1836) and Samuel Slater (1768–1835) established the first waterpowered cotton mill in the United States in 1790. Brown was a businessman and philanthropist (Brown University bears his name) who provided the financing. Slater was born in England and learned about textile machinery there. He came to the United States in disguise because the emigration of people with knowledge of the textile-manufacturing process was forbidden in an effort to retain a monopoly for Great Britain. Unable to obtain models of British machinery even by smuggling them in, Slater recreated all the necessary machinery by a remarkable feat of memory.

Textile manufacturing on a larger scale was developed by Francis Cabot Lowell (1775–1817), Nathan Appleton (1779–1861) and Patrick Tracy Jackson (1780–1847). Lowell was the leader but all three exemplified the successful American merchant turned manufacturer. Lowell went to England in 1810 where he studied textile operations. When he returned he constructed the first power loom in America from some drawings and his memory. Appleton's capital came from shipping. In an account he later wrote of the textile enterprise, he said:

> It was the Americans who first introduced the manufacture of heavy goods by the application of the least amount of labor to the greatest quantity of raw material, thus producing a description of goods cheaper to the consumer than any heretofore existing.

Jackson, Lowell's brother-in-law, was a sea captain by the time he reached his early twenties and retired from the sea at the age of twenty-eight.

The three partners built their mill at Waltham, Massachusetts, in 1814, and Lowell was chiefly responsible for making this the first in which all the operations involved in converting cotton to cloth were performed in one building. In need of more waterpower, the mills were moved to the Merrimac River, and the city of Lowell, Massachusetts, grew up around them. Here, too, the boardinghouse system was made famous. Most of the factory hands were girls from the farms and small towns of New England. The company erected boardinghouses for them, where they were carefully chaperoned. No saloons were allowed in Lowell and the girls went frequently to church. The system was wholly paternalistic and class distinctions were obvious in the different quality of housing provided for employees up the scale from unskilled workers to managers. Nevertheless, many girls flocked to such company towns. They stayed a few years, saved up money for their dowries and then went back home to be married. Wages in the early textile mills were probably better than in most occupations outside of factories, but the girls worked seventy hours a week for a wage of $2.00.

The woolen industry grew also, especially after Merino sheep were brought to America. This was done in 1802 by David Humphreys (1752–1818), a diplomat and a poet. He brought in a hundred of this breed, developed in Spain and noted for its long life and heavy fleece. Humphreys built a woolen mill in Connecticut with its own paternalistic community, and he used orphan boys as mill hands.

As with textiles, the iron industry was stimulated when the war cut off supplies from Great Britain. Iron mining and iron smelting were carried on in colonial times in Massachusetts, Connecticut, New York and New Jersey. Iron manufacturing moved westward, reaching Pittsburgh before 1820. Until the war, some pig iron was exported to England, where it was turned into finished products. With the rise of industry in America, the manufacturing of machines made of iron —for textile plants and a little later for steam engines—began at home. There was always a steady demand for pots and pans, nails, wire and other common products. Before factories took over such work, the local blacksmith manufactured these goods, along with shoeing horses. More coal was produced in Virginia than in any other state in 1820, but the mining industry was growing in Pennsylvania.

Shipping and the import-export trade contributed significantly to the American economy. The prosperity, or lack of it, of overseas commerce in the early nineteenth century depended on the political and military situation in different parts of the world. Wars in Europe stimulated demand for American products, but the efforts of both sides to keep shipping out of the hands of the other made difficulties for the American merchant marine. The War of 1812 was the low point. After its end foreign trade spurted, but an excess of goods and unsettled business conditions brought a noticeable decrease in imports and exports by 1819. The port of New York continued to forge ahead, but Philadelphia, Baltimore, Boston and New Orleans were busy too. The Black Ball line between Liverpool and New York was established in 1818, the first of the packet lines. These ships, instead of waiting for a full cargo, sailed regularly on dates announced in advance and they proved to be very successful.

While America's natural shipping relations were with the West Indies and Europe, trade with the Far East began with the voyage of a single ship in 1784. By the early nineteenth century American ships were swarming all over the Pacific, visiting Hawaii and the Fiji Islands, as well as the coast and rivers of China where dealings were carried on with merchants and government officials. Goods for different markets were shipped and reshipped in the course of long voyages. The Chinese provided an excellent market for furs from the American northwest and for ginseng plants dug up in New York and New England. The Chinese thought ginseng had miraculous medicinal properties. Tea came to America in large quantities, along with porcelain, painted screens and carved ivory. Sandalwood was a valuable cargo, as was pepper. American ships and exporters handled 7,500,000 pounds of Sumatra pepper in 1805, almost the whole crop of the year. Salem, Massachusetts, was the home port of more ships trading with the Far East than any other, and took on a personality shaped by this situation. Crew members and officers were very young and many an American youth laid the basis of his fortune on such voyages. One ship sailed with a captain twenty years old and a first mate of nineteen, while on another ship all thirteen crew members later became masters of their own vessels.

Whaling was a maritime industry with its own mechanics and economics. After a setback during the War of 1812, Americans again took the lead and for nearly forty years after 1820 sailed all over the north and south Pacific in search of whales. Voyages lasted as long as four years and were both profitable and dangerous. Herman Melville's *Moby Dick* is the classic account in novel form of life on a whaler. New Bedford, Massachusetts, was the foremost whaling port.

An inventive businessman, Frederic Tudor of Boston, went into the business of shipping New England ice to warmer regions. Tudor's first shipment sailed to the West Indies in 1806, but it was fifteen years before the venture was profitable. New techniques were devised for cutting ice and for storing it so that, in effect, the New England climate became an article of export. Havana and New Orleans received such ice in 1821, and by 1833 ice was being shipped to India.

Federal government participation in banking in the United States began with the chartering by Congress in 1791 of the Bank of the United States. The government subscribed some of the capital and the bank acted as fiscal agent for the government. The bank was part of Hamilton's overall plan for establishing a sound economy for the new nation. Jeffersonians opposed the bank on the grounds that the Constitution did not give the government power to establish such an institution, and that it would favor business over agrarian interests. The bank was a financial success but when its charter expired in 1811, the Republicans, with Madison as president, were in power and refused to grant a new charter. Soon thereafter the War of 1812, with its problems of government finance, showed how useful a central bank could be. The government had a very difficult time borrowing money to finance the war.

By 1816 the Republicans were ready to sponsor the chartering of a second Bank of the United States, this time with capital of $35,-000,000. The head office remained in Philadelphia, while twenty-five branches were opened around the country. The bank's first management was inefficient but its standing and credit were restored after 1819 when Langdon Cheves (1776–1857) became its president. A South Carolina lawyer and one of the original War Hawks, Cheves was elected speaker of the House of Representatives in 1814. He was succeeded as bank president in 1823 by Nicholas Biddle (1786–1844), who had graduated from Princeton at the age of fifteen and had served in diplomatic posts abroad. At home Biddle was connected with the leading magazine, the *Port Folio,* and edited it after 1812. He edited the journals of the Lewis and Clark expedition in 1814.

Other banks, chartered by the states, grew in numbers and spread westward. The absence of a Bank of the United States from 1811 to 1816 accelerated their growth, and they increased from 88 to 146 in this period. In 1801 there had been about thirty banks. The leading private banker was Stephen Girard (1750–1831), who was born in France and settled in America in 1776 as a shipowner and merchant. When the charter of the first Bank of the United States was not renewed, he set up his own institution and helped Madison's administration float loans to finance the War of 1812.

The Constitution provided for the establishment of a national currency and the Mint Act of 1792 made the dollar the basic unit of value. It was some time, though, before enough United States money was circulating to satisfy the nation's needs. No gold was being mined as yet in the country and the generally unfavorable balance of trade meant that gold and silver had to be sent out of the country to pay for imports. As a result, foreign coins circulated widely for a good many years longer than expected to make up for the shortage.

From the beginning in 1789, duties were levied on imports but the purpose was to raise revenue for the Federal government, not to protect American products. The tariff, in fact, was the chief support of federal finances until the Civil War, bringing in about 80 per cent of all government revenue most of the time. In some periods, customs duties were so plentiful that the problem was what to do with the surplus after the expenses of the government had been met.

After the War of 1812, in an atmosphere of heightened nationalistic feeling, the tariff became entangled with politics as a part of the debate over the American System. The first tariff law passed by Congress that was admittedly intended to keep foreign goods from competing with American manufactures was that of 1816. The heart of it was a rate of 25 per cent of value placed on cotton and woolen goods and iron products from overseas. The only serious opposition came from the New England shipping interests.

Eight years later, with all the 1824 presidential candidates favoring the principle of a protective tariff, a new bill was enacted which raised the duties again. The special interests of groups and sections showed up very clearly. New England was divided: manufacturers were for higher rates, the shippers were opposed. The wool-growers wanted a high duty on the importation of raw wool; the manufacturers of woolen goods wanted a low duty on raw wool and a high duty on manufactured woolens. As an exporter of raw materials and an importer of manufactured goods, the South was almost unanimous in its opposition to high tariffs. For example, southern representatives fought duties on woolen goods because the South used a great deal of such items as clothing for its slaves.

The first banking crisis and the first serious economic depression of the young nation occurred in 1819, brought about by a number of factors. Booming conditions after the War of 1812 encouraged a great deal of over-expansion in business, agriculture, banking and land speculation. The demand for American farm products then dropped as Europe recovered from the Napoleonic wars. The price of cotton rose to thirty-three cents a pound in 1818 and then slumped to eight cents the next year. Cotton planters, meanwhile, had been buying land at inflated prices. In the West, too, farmers added to their acreage at inflated prices. Purchasers of public lands were behind in their payments to the government to the extent of nearly $22,000,000.

The financial crisis was precipitated by weaknesses in the banking system. When the second Bank of the United States was rescued from its early mismanagement, it was partly at the expense of other banks. These banks, especially in the West and South, had issued far too much paper money and had extended far too much credit, largely in the form of mortgages on land. When the Bank of the United

States tightened its rules in dealing with these banks, they found themselves in serious trouble and many failed at the expense of their creditors and depositors. The depression lasted about three years and during that time the country saw such unusual sights as soup kitchens in New York and other eastern cities. Some states passed laws to prevent or delay the foreclosure of mortgages. Several states had the good sense to adopt stricter banking laws for the future.

Skilled labor was scarce in the early years of the century. Most people lived on farms so that the pool of urban workers to draw on was small. And all the time the West was luring potential factory hands to try their luck as pioneers. Employers often advertised for skilled workmen. Philadelphia, Baltimore and Charleston newspapers in 1803 carried advertisements for stonecutters inserted by contractors erecting New York's city hall. The advertisements assured the workers that although there was some yellow fever in New York they need not worry about it. The trend in wages was generally upward. Unskilled labor was paid ninety cents a day or less in 1800, a dollar or so by 1820. Skilled labor around 1800 received one to two dollars a day, although men with special skills such as ships' carpenters or tailors were better paid. If wages were low, so were prices. One could buy about ten pounds of meat for a dollar, or several gallons of whiskey, or nearly an acre of public land. Hours of labor were long, usually at least twelve hours a day, six days a week, even for children. Most of the child labor was found in the textile mills of New England. In Massachusetts in 1820, 45 per cent of the workers in the cotton mills were children, as were 55 per cent in Rhode Island.

Labor unions in the modern sense did not exist, but even before 1800 there were organizations of craftsmen, such as the cordwainers (shoemakers) in Philadelphia and the printers in New York. These trade societies were concerned with internal interests, such as insurance programs and protection against too many apprentices entering a particular trade, as well as in getting better terms from their employers. A strike—or "turn-out"—of the Philadelphia shoemakers in 1806 resulted in a legal setback for union labor. No legislation existed concerning the rights and duties of unions, but under British common law when a union as a body went on strike, its members were guilty of conspiracy in restraint of trade. An anti-union judge declared the shoemakers' strike was "pregnant with public mischief and private injury." In this case and five others up to 1815, the unions were found guilty four times. The depression of 1819 had an adverse effect on the unions, but when prosperity returned the unions became more active. For the first time textile-mill workers, of whom by 1820 there were 100,000, organized. This in turn led to the first strike by women workers in 1824, at Pawtucket, Rhode Island. By this time unions were agitating for a ten-hour day and in some cases they succeeded.

Although the United States took its first steps toward becoming an industrial nation, the first quarter of the century saw it not only continuing as primarily an agricultural country, but also experiencing a great expansion of its farming areas and products. This growth had three causes. The amount of land under cultivation increased, especially in the West, including the Mississippi Valley, but also in such parts of the South as Alabama and Mississippi. Farming also began to be more specialized. Finally, scientific advances in farming methods and technological advances in farm machinery increased production per acre and per hour of labor spent in the fields.

In 1800 tobacco was the South's most important crop and, in fact, the nation's most valuable export. However, it declined steadily in importance because of competition from other countries, and land exhaustion, and because cotton became a more profitable crop. One major impetus for the switch to cotton came from a Yankee, Eli Whitney (1765–1825). While a tutor in the South in 1793, Whitney in ten days constructed a model of the first cotton gin, a device for separating the cotton fiber from the seed. Prior to his invention, a slave needed about a day to clean one pound of cotton. With the cotton gin, which was soon improved, one slave could handle fifty pounds a day. As a result, the amount of cotton grown could be greatly increased and so, from the slaveholder's point of view, more slaves than ever were needed.

In the first five years of the century, the cotton crop averaged 59,600,000 pounds annually, of which about 56 per cent was exported. By the 1821–25 period, production had increased more than three times, to 209,000,000 pounds a year, and almost 73 per cent of it was being exported. The South also produced sugarcane in Louisiana, and rice in South Carolina and Georgia, but more and more acreage was put into cotton, especially as cotton-growing spread west and south, to Alabama and Mississippi.

The greatest expansion in the number of farmers and of farms took place west of the Alleghenies, mostly in the old Northwest Territory north of the Ohio River. This area became the largest food-producing region, and fed the East, particularly after roads and canals made it economical to send such products as corn and livestock to market there. Corn was the staple crop, and its use to feed livestock made hog raising a major farm activity also. Before better transportation routes opened up, much corn went east in the form of whiskey, a less bulky item of freight. Meat packing rose to be an important industry in the region by 1818, with Cincinnati as its center. Kentucky, from its earliest days of settlement, grew hemp as a major crop.

Americans were wasteful in their use of the land. With so much land there for the taking, it was easier to use up a plot and move on than to conserve its fertility. In addition, scientific knowledge about soil, crops, livestock and fertilizers developed slowly. Even before the nineteenth century, though, the scientific aspects of agriculture attracted serious attention. Washington and Jefferson were but two of the leading figures of the time who made a study of farming methods. More farmers every year learned the wisdom of rotating crops and of using fertilizers. New crops were introduced, such as the Irish potato which by 1800 was already a significant addition to farming in Maine and on Long Island. Livestock was improved by bringing in better breeds from Europe. Henry Clay, for example, introduced Hereford cattle into Kentucky in 1817. Alderneys and Guernseys, well-known British dairy breeds, were imported in the 1820's.

Farm equipment was improved and made more efficient. Jethro Wood (1774–1834), an inventor and farmer, patented an improved plow in 1819. Made of cast iron, it had easily replaceable parts and a more efficiently shaped moldboard for turning the soil. Both the cradle and the horse hayrake came into use about 1820. The cradle was an improvement over the sickle for cutting and gathering grain. The horse hayrake could do the work of eight to ten men. As crops increased, the processing of them became an industrial operation rather than something each farmer did for himself. By 1800 there were mills that could make flour of 100,000 bushels of grain a year.

More opportunities were provided for securing useful agricultural information. The first magazine for farmers, *The American Farmer,* began publication in Baltimore in 1819. Within two months the *Plough Boy* was being published in Albany, New York, and, in 1822, *The New England Farmer* appeared. The first institution for the teaching of agriculture, the Gardiner Lyceum, was established in 1822 in Gardiner, Maine. Elkanah Watson (1758–1842) was the pioneer of the agricultural fair which developed into one of America's favorite institutions and recreations, the county fair. He exhibited two Merino sheep in the center of Pittsfield, Massachusetts, in 1807, and three years later convinced his neighbors they should join him in a larger exhibition.

The state of agriculture was improving, but in the early years of the century a farmer's life, especially on the western frontier, was not an easy one. The prospect of taking up one's own acres in virgin territory at comparatively little expense could be most enticing. The reality of settling land, especially in wooded country, was another matter. A man, working hard, could clear an acre a month, so that several years went by at best before all of a hundred-acre farm was cultivable. Settlers in rural areas also faced the prospect of loneliness with few neighbors anywhere near. Many families that left the East, where land was already worn out and where, at times, jobs were hard to find, discovered life no better on the frontier. Some of these pioneers gave up and came back East. Always, however, more men and women were ready to try a new life, and enough of them kept moving westward so that it sometimes seemed the whole nation was on the march.

7   *Transportation—Technology*

TRANSPORTATION AND POWER—these were the two vital needs of a rapidly growing nation spread over a large territory. The needs were met most spectacularly by the invention of the steamboat, and by the adaptation of the steam engine to other purposes, such as operating factory machinery. But the newness of the steamboat should not overshadow the importance of road and bridge building, which provided badly needed arteries for the flow of raw materials, finished products and business communications. In addition, the canal and the railroad were almost ready to play their roles by the end of the first quarter of the nineteenth century.

The emphasis in this era was on getting things done, on making machinery work even if one didn't know all the principles behind it. Engineers were in short supply. There were some trained engineers who had emigrated from Europe, others were self-taught, with on-the-job training. The center of American engineering education was the United States Military Academy at West Point, established in 1802. At that time West Point was the headquarters of the Corps of Engineers, and until the War of 1812 moved Congress to expand the institution, the emphasis was on engineering. In 1819 a former superintendent of the academy started a "scientific and military" school in Vermont which became Norwich University, the first civilian engineering school. Stephen Van Rensselaer, who played an important role in the building of the Erie Canal, founded a technical school at Troy, New York, in 1824, which became Rensselaer Polytechnic Institute.

Inventors in both Europe and America had experimented with steam-propelled boats in the eighteenth century. James Rumsey of Maryland demonstrated a steamboat on the Potomac River in 1787. John Fitch built one in 1790 that traveled at eight miles an hour and ran successfully between Philadelphia and Burlington. To Robert Fulton, however, goes the credit for building and operating a steamboat that was a practical commercial venture.

Fulton (1765–1815), born in Pennsylvania, was a man of assorted talents. First an expert gunsmith, he turned to painting and achieved a measure of success in England and France. He next worked on such inventions as a submarine and an underwater torpedo. Fulton lived abroad for about twenty years and during that time witnessed the trials of a steamboat in Scotland, and experimented with one himself on the Seine River in France. When he returned to the United States, Robert R. Livingston of New York, who was farsighted enough to have acquired a grant giving him a monopoly on steamboat navigation in New York waters, engaged Fulton to build a ship. Livingston (1746–1813) was active in government and politics, first as a Federalist and then, after a falling out with Hamilton, as a Jeffersonian. He administered the oath of office to President George Washington in 1789 and was America's chief negotiator in France of the Louisiana Purchase.

Fulton went to work and on August 7, 1807, his ship, the *Clermont,* was ready for an extended test. The ship was 150 feet long but only 13 feet wide, and had two paddle wheels, 15 feet in diameter, one on each side of the hull. The steam power was supplied by a British engine. The trip from New York to Albany and back was a complete success—the *Clermont* steamed up the Hudson in thirty-two hours running time and back in thirty. Fulton and Livingston extended their operations and the age of steam travel on water had arrived.

The steamboat soon appeared on the Mississippi River and its large tributaries, where its value was even greater than on eastern rivers, since in the West distances were longer and currents were stronger. When the Louisiana Purchase doubled the size of the United States, Jefferson worried that the nation might have to split up because of the distances involved. The steamboat was one answer to this problem. Fulton and Livingston established a shipyard in Pittsburgh in 1811, and built the first steamship on the western waters, the *New Orleans*, which in the winter of 1812 voyaged down the Ohio and Mississippi to New Orleans. The engines for the boat were built in the United States by Nicholas Roosevelt (1767–1845). Roosevelt, from whose branch of the family President Theodore Roosevelt was descended, had a machine shop, the Soho Works, near Newark, New Jersey, that was as advanced as any in the country.

Fulton's type of boat, however, did not do well going upstream against the strong current of the Mississippi. This problem was partly solved by Henry M. Shreve (1785–1851) who built and launched the *Washington* at Wheeling, Virginia, in 1817. Shreve's boat was a prototype of what developed into the familiar Mississippi riverboat. Copying the flat-bottomed keelboat in use for so long on the river, Shreve built a shallow-hulled craft that was less likely to get stuck on sandbars. He put the engine on the deck and placed a second deck over it. Out of this idea grew the palatial boats that carried freight and passengers up and down the western waters.

The number of steamboats increased every year. By 1817 there were seventeen in the West, and in five years sixty more were added. Twenty-five miles an hour downstream and sixteen up was the rate of the boats by 1825. As speeds went up, fares fell. In 1818 the fare was about $100 to $125 to go from New Orleans to Louisville; by 1825 the rate was down to $50.

These western boats used high-pressure steam engines which often blew up. One reason for this was the compulsion of the daring captains and proud owners to race each other with the safety valve on the engine tied down, so that power would not be reduced when the danger point of steam pressure was reached. In the first half of the century as many as 30 per cent of the boats built were lost in accidents. In agitating for an inspection of local steamboats, a Philadelphia newspaper in 1817 reported an accident on the Mississippi in which the steam "exploded and scattered such abundance of boiling water, that eleven persons were scalded to death and many others dangerously wounded."

The use of steamboats spread quickly to other bodies of water. The first boat on Lake Erie, *Walk in the Water,* appeared in 1818 and made the trip between Buffalo and Detroit in nine days. The next year a steamboat went up the Missouri River from St. Louis to Council Bluffs, Iowa. Regular service between New York and New Orleans was established in 1820. The first crossing of the Atlantic Ocean using steam power took place in 1819 when the *Savannah,* sailing from that city in Georgia, made the trip to Liverpool in twenty-nine days, eleven hours. The *Savannah,* though, was primarily a sailing ship and, as remained customary for some time, used its steam power only when winds failed, in this case for about ninety hours.

Oliver Evans (1755–1819) deserves equal place with Robert Fulton in the history of steam power. Evans had invented several machines for use in flour mills, and in 1807 he established the Mars Iron Works where he built fifty steam engines. He also invented the first steam-powered dredge, but his most important contribution to technology was the high-pressure steam engine. The steam engine James Watt had developed in Great Britain produced only a few pounds of pressure per square inch. Evans designed his engine to use forty to sixty pounds of pressure per square inch, and to apply the power directly to the piston instead of first putting the steam into a condenser. This made for a simpler, cheaper and more powerful engine, one that could conquer the Mississippi. Evans also experimented with a steam carriage to run on roads, and in 1812 predicted that eventually "carriages propelled by steam will be in general use, as well for the transportation of passengers as goods, travelling at the rate of fifteen miles an hour."

This possibility, in terms of the railroad, was already being investigated by John Stevens (1749–1838) of New Jersey. After inheriting a large estate from his father, he turned his attention to steamboats and almost paralleled the work of Fulton. Between 1806 and 1808 he built the *Phoenix,* which was intended to be a seagoing ship but was used as a shuttle between Philadelphia and Trenton beginning in 1809. Two years later he operated a steam ferry between New York and Hoboken. Beginning in 1810, Stevens devoted his efforts to making the steam locomotive and the railroad a practical means of transportation. In 1815 the state of New Jersey granted him the first charter in the country for a railroad, which was to be built between the Delaware and Raritan rivers. Ten years passed, however, before Stevens operated a locomotive, the first to run on rails in the United States. His "Steam Waggon" was sixteen feet long and guests at his estate rode it around a circular track at the rate of twelve miles an hour. Thus, as the quarter century ended, the nation was on the verge of another advance in transportation, one that would link the sprawling nation together with bands of iron.

From the earliest times, American settlers had roads of sorts, if nothing more than Indian trails. By the early eighteenth century, a road ran from Massachusetts to Georgia, although it was not any great pleasure to bump over it. As the nation grew and the population spread westward, more and better roads were needed. Rivers did not always run in the most practical direction and some of them were only partially navigable. None could be used for the vital connections needed between the East and the West, separated as they were by mountains. Accordingly, the early nineteenth century saw a great deal of road-building. Some roads were built by local authorities, turnpikes by private companies, and the National Road and some military roads by the Federal government.

Most of the important roads constructed in the early nineteenth century, except for the National Road, were turnpikes. These were built by private companies, under a charter from a state which authorized them to charge tolls for the use of the road. Turnpike companies were in high favor for a while, but they were never as profitable as those who organized them and invested in them hoped. Turnpike building began before 1800, with the first important one being the Philadelphia to Lancaster Turnpike, completed in 1794. The New England and the Middle Atlantic states led in turnpike building, and the only important southern turnpike was that between Charleston and Columbia, South Carolina. In New York, by 1821, about 4,000 miles of turnpikes were built by 278 different companies. By that same year, Pennsylvania had authorized 146 turnpikes. The Pennsylvania Turnpike, from Philadelphia to Pittsburgh, was an important artery and was kept in good repair, unlike some of the roads. One Philadelphia business by 1825 sent more than 200 wagons a year over this turnpike. Baltimore continued to be the third largest city, in part because seven different turnpikes ended there, thus making it a hub for commerce from all directions. During the War of 1812, when the British blockaded the Atlantic Coast, it was estimated that 20,000 oxen were being used to haul 4,000 freight wagons over the route from Boston to Augusta, Georgia, most of which was turnpike. The turnpike boom ended in the late 1820's.

Road travel was expensive, especially for freight. The average charge around the country was $10 per ton per hundred miles. Turnpikes in New Jersey charged a cent a mile for each horse using the roads. Passenger travel cost about six cents a mile and twenty-five cents for a four-wheeled carriage. One could drive sheep along a turnpike for three cents a dozen.

The National Road was the first large-scale highway construction project of the Federal government, and the only one in the first quarter of the century. Although authorized by Congress in 1806, actual construction of the road did not start until 1811 and the war soon interfered. Little was accomplished until 1815 when work began in earnest. The road started at Cumberland, Maryland, which was already linked to Baltimore, 135 miles east. As conceived, the National Road was to run all the way to the Mississippi River. The first section, to Wheeling, Virginia, was completed in 1818, and proved its value in short order. Freight was hauled by six-horse teams and the time to Baltimore was cut in half, from eight to four days. Five thousand wagons a year were arriving in Wheeling by 1822 and for a while the citizens of that city had visions of it becoming more important than Pittsburgh, but they were disappointed in the end. This first section of the National Road was well constructed of stone and gravel. Stone bridges with graceful arches carried it over streams, and iron mileposts told the traveler his location. The road slowly pushed westward, and by 1838 the government had spent nearly $7,-000,000 on it. For many years it was a main route of the ever-flowing river of men, women and children moving westward to settle. Eastbound, it was the most heavily used and most economical land route for the produce of the West to reach eastern markets.

On foot and on horseback, in wagons and in stage coaches, people traveled over the National Road and other highways. Horses and oxen did the hauling of vehicles; sheep and cattle were driven to market; and pioneer families carried along with them furniture, equipment, chickens and dogs. The best of the vehicles for hauling heavy loads was the Conestoga Wagon, first built about 1725 in Pennsylvania and named for the Conestoga Valley, which in turn took its name from an Indian tribe. This type of wagon had a distinctive shape because the wagon box curved up at each end so that freight would not shift position easily on hills. The large white covers, of hempen homespun or, later, canvas, curved in the same way and gave a graceful, sailing-ship effect. The larger Conestoga wagons were pulled by six horses and carried up to eight tons of freight. The drivers of these wagons are credited with having developed the custom of driving on the right-hand side of the road. The teamster of a Conestoga rode the left wheelhorse, or the "lazyboard," which pulled out from the side of the wagon. He could then see oncoming traffic better if he kept his wagon to the right.

For passengers, the stage coach provided the first-class accommodations of the day, although such travel was most uncomfortable by later standards. Stage coaches required relatively wide and stable roads, so they were just coming into common use at the start of the century. Stage coaches of different sizes carried eight to fourteen passengers, plus baggage, mail and the driver. One or more passengers had to ride on top with the driver. Building stage coaches became both an industry and an art. The builders of Albany and Troy, New York, and Concord, New Hampshire, were well known for their skill. The Concord coach, especially, was held in high regard. It was handsomely shaped and had silk upholstery with oak paneling. Oil paintings sometimes decorated the door panels. The outsides were gaily painted in such colors as scarlet and yellow. The coaches were suspended on leather straps which ran lengthwise and provided the "spring." While this construction made the coaches more comfortable than freight wagons, it nevertheless allowed a good deal of jolting and swaying. More than one traveler suffered the equivalent of seasickness.

By 1800 a coach left New York for Philadelphia every weekday, taking nearly two days for the journey. A stage-coach line to run from the east to Pittsburgh was established in 1804, and all during the quarter century lines were reaching out to farther points, north, south and west. The average fare a passenger paid was five cents a mile. For this, he was badly shaken up if the road was a poor one, for twelve to eighteen hours a day. In the summer the coachman might cover forty miles and in the winter probably twenty-five a day.

Canals were a growing part of the transportation system, increasing in number and length rapidly as the quarter century ended. A few canals, mostly quite short, were built before 1800, but the building of the Erie Canal in New York State, starting in 1817, touched off the boom. Like most canals the Erie was built by a state government rather than by private companies. The chief sponsor and enthusiastic supporter of the Erie Canal was De Witt Clinton. He was named canal commissioner as early as 1810, and while governor between 1817 and 1821 he continued to supervise its construction. The Erie Canal ran 350 miles from the Hudson River at Albany to Lake Erie, and was opened a section at a time. The first boat on it sailed from Rome to Utica in the fall of 1819. The whole canal was officially opened in late October, 1825. Goods and people could then travel all the way from Lake Erie, and the other lakes west of it, to the Atlantic Ocean at New York harbor.

Almost immediately all of New York prospered from the canal traffic. Large quantities of western produce floated along the canal, since it cost only about one tenth as much to ship by canal boat as by horse and wagon. The Erie carried 218,000 tons of freight in its first year. Work began on other canals, such as the Delaware and Hudson, in 1825, to connect those two rivers. That same year saw the start of the Miami and Erie Canal, to join the Ohio at Cincinnati with Lake Erie at Toledo, and the Ohio and Erie Canal from Portsmouth on the river to Cleveland on the lake. The Champlain Canal in New York was completed in 1823. Many canals were finished just in time to face railroad competition, which they could not meet for long.

Roads required bridges and, a little later, so did canals and railroads. Consequently, bridge-building technology was forced to keep pace with the growth of other transportation facilities. The country was fortunate in having a number of bridge engineers, mostly self-taught, who planned and experimented successfully. In some cases they arrived independently at technical solutions that were known elsewhere. Timothy Palmer (1775–1821) was the engineer responsible for the Permanent Bridge over the Schuylkill River in Philadelphia, built in 1800–05. It was a trussed-arch bridge, built of timber. A truss bridge had a framework of wooden beams built in a lattice work that gave the effect of a series of triangles. The Permanent Bridge, like most wooden bridges, was roofed, not to protect travelers, but to protect the material of the bridge itself from the elements.

Theodore Burr (1771?–1822) built his first major bridge across the Hudson at Waterford, New York, in 1803–04. It had a shingle roof and stood for 105 years before it burned down. Burr's most spectacular achievement was the construction of a bridge over the Susquehanna River near Lancaster, Pennsylvania, with a single span of 360 feet. He chose to build it in the middle of the winter of 1814–15 by working from the ice while the river was frozen. He got away with his gamble with the weather but, ironically, two years later ice swept the bridge away. Louis Wernwag (1769–1843), born in Germany, in 1812 constructed the Colossus Bridge over the Schuylkill at Fairmount Park, Philadelphia, with a span of 340 feet which then was the longest wooden road bridge ever built. In twenty-seven years of practice, Wernwag constructed twenty-nine bridges.

Ithiel Town (1784–1844) trained at an architectural school in Boston. In 1820 he patented a form of truss bridge with a diamond pattern of closely spaced diagonals. Since this was simple to construct and did not call for any special materials, he earned a large amount of money in royalties from his patent. In an article written in 1821 he considered the problem of rigid iron bridges fifteen years before any were built in the United States. Although the principle of the suspension bridge had been known for centuries, James Finley (1762–1828) of Pennsylvania invented the iron-chain suspension bridge with a deck suitable for traffic. He built his first bridge in 1801 on the Uniontown Turnpike, where he had a $600 contract to erect a bridge with a seventy-foot span.

A number of other Americans and a French family contributed to the technological revolution that accelerated during the nineteenth century. Eli Whitney, after inventing the cotton gin, returned north to Connecticut and in 1798 established a firearms factory where he proposed to make muskets with interchangeable parts—the basis of modern mass production. Whitney received a government contract for 10,000 muskets to be produced in twenty-eight months. He fell far behind, so he went to Washington in early 1801 where he demonstrated to President Adams, Vice-President Jefferson and others that the idea worked. He received an extension of time, but it was 1809 before he completed the contract and his net profit for a decade's work was only $2,500. Seth Thomas (1785–1859), also in Connecticut, worked along the same lines as Whitney. As early as 1807 Thomas began manufacturing standardized clock parts in quantity and assembling identical clocks from them. Thomas Blanchard (1788–1864) invented a machine that would carve out wooden gunstocks. It was in use in the Springfield Armory from 1821 on.

Nathaniel Bowditch (1773–1838), of Massachusetts, had no formal schooling after he was ten, but became the most useful mathematician of the time. After he went to sea in 1795 he discovered about 8,000 errors in what was then the best guide to navigation. His own work, *The New American Practical Navigator* (1802), became the worldwide standard. When he died all the seafaring nations flew their ships' flags at half-mast.

The Du Pont family established itself in America in this period. Pierre Samuel Du Pont (1739–1817) left France in 1799 because of the revolution. He became acquainted with Jefferson and after his return to France in 1802, Jefferson sought his aid with the Louisiana Purchase. Du Pont was an economist of note, and his theories had some influence on the American president. His son, Eleuthère Irénée Du Pont (1772–1834) entered the French royal gunpowder works as a young man and there studied under Antoine Lavoisier, one of the founders of modern chemistry. Du Pont emigrated to the United States and set up a powder mill of his own in 1802 near Wilmington, Delaware. He improved gunpowder and his mill was an important supply source for the American forces in the War of 1812.

All this time a variety of developments—some important, some merely adding to the comfort of everyday living—were taking place. By 1812 Pittsburgh became the leading glass-manufacturing city with five plants in operation. A few years later American manufacturers worked out a technique for producing pressed glassware which lowered costs and made the product available to more people. Refrigeration on a large scale, using natural ice, began near the start of the century. The first American refrigerator was patented in 1803, a double-walled cabinet with a partitioned section for the ice. At first ice was expensive, and only 180 tons were sold commercially in 1803. Baltimore in 1816 was the first American city to use gas lighting. The country had plenty of natural gas but the gas was in the West, away from the centers of population. Fredonia, a small town in western New York, had gas lighting in the 1820's. And, although false teeth were not new, the first patent for dentures was issued in 1822 to C. M. Graham.

8   The West: Old and New

FROM THE VERY BEGINNING in the seventeenth century, a vital factor in the settlement of the North American colonies was a frontier that constantly marched westward. The frontier was both a physical fact and a dream.

By 1800 the physical frontier—and the people—had been on the move for nearly two centuries. The first difficult barrier was the Appalachian Mountain chain, consisting of several mountain groupings running southwest from the St. Lawrence Valley to the gulf coast plain in Alabama. In the history of the settlement of the land east of the Mississippi River, the two ranges that mattered were the Allegheny Mountains and the Blue Ridge Mountains. The Alleghenies run from northern Pennsylvania through Maryland and western Virginia, with a western plateau that reaches into Kentucky and eastern Ohio. The Blue Ridge Mountains run from northwestern Maryland, southwestward through Virginia and North Carolina into Georgia.

By the treaty that ended the American Revolution and gave the colonies their independence, the new United States extended westward to the Mississippi River and northward to Canada along the line of the Great Lakes. Even before that time, some Americans had tried to force the mountain barrier but were mostly restrained by British orders and by hostile Indians allied with the British. Independence removed British rule, but not the danger of the Indians or the difficulty of travel in an almost uncharted land. The movement over the mountains gained momentum nevertheless. The Cumberland Gap, near where Virginia, Kentucky and Tennessee meet, was the main point of entry into the trans-Allegheny region. Enough people moved in, chiefly from the southern states, so that both Kentucky and Tennessee were admitted to the union before 1800.

Before the territory over the mountains was well settled, the Louisiana Purchase of 1803 added an unknown region of broad rivers, endless grassy plains and high mountains. Explorers and trappers had crossed the Mississippi and probed the new domain before the purchase. Now that the American flag flew over this region, it was only a matter of time before restless Americans pushed the frontier line nearer to the Pacific coast.

That was the reality of the frontier—mountains and rivers to be crossed, territory to be explored, land to be settled, farms to be established and towns and cities to be built. But there was also a frontier of dream and myth. The New World from the time of its discovery was a land of hope. In this almost untouched wilderness Eden, man could start over. He would put aside the burdens and mistakes of the European past and become a better man in a better world. As the Atlantic coastal area was settled, though, the people and their civilization resembled in many ways the people and civilization they had left behind in Europe. But there was a new frontier over the mountains, and life there would surely be both different and better. Thus the myth of the western frontier as something that changed people, even while they changed it, was firmly established. The myth still did not die when, at last, the frontier reached the Pacific Ocean.

On the more practical side, the increase in the nation's territory and the spread of people raised the question of whether one government could bind together such a geographical expanse. Some men thought that the land west of the Appalachians would become a separate nation. When Louisiana was added, there was talk of the Rocky Mountains as the final barrier, and that the remaining area west to the Pacific would have to be under its own government. Gradually, however, the idea that the nation's destiny was to spread over this land—in fact over the whole continent—became part of the dream of a great and unique future in store for the American people as they continued toward the west. A popular Fourth of July toast in 1815 was: "The Eagle of the United States—may she extend her wings from the Atlantic to the Pacific; and fixing her talons on the Isthmus of Darien, stretch her beak to the Northern Pole."

During the early years of the nation, more practical matters had to be dealt with. Seven of the original thirteen states, through their colonial charters, had laid claims (often overlapping) to land over the mountains. In a statesmanlike move, they gave up those claims to the central government. The Northwest Ordinance of 1787 established a precedent, and an excellent one, for dealing with unsettled frontier areas. It provided that the land north of the Ohio and east of the Mississippi—the Old Northwest—be divided into three to five territories. It also spelled out how these territories could gradually become states, on an equal footing with those already in the union. Citizens who moved from a state into this area would in the end lose no rights or privileges.

The transfer of this land also meant that the Federal government was in the real-estate business, and had to establish a policy for turning land over to settlers. Several different laws passed between 1800 and 1820 spelled out how a person could acquire some of the public lands. Prices were low, the law of 1800 set a rate of $2 an acre, which could be paid over four years, with a minimum purchase of 320 acres. The generous credit provisions in the laws, intended to encourage individual purchase of farmlands, also encouraged speculation. As time went on, many purchasers fell behind in their payments. Over 19,000,000 acres had been sold by 1820, but nearly a third had not been paid for. A new law in 1820 reduced the price to $1.25 an acre, and put the sale on a cash basis. The minimum acreage a man could buy was also reduced, to eighty acres.

The population of the Old Northwest grew steadily, increasing more rapidly after the war of 1812 than before. In 1800 there were 51,000 settlers; in 1810, 272,000; and by 1820, almost 800,000. The newcomers were mostly Americans moving from the East, although after the war the number of immigrants arriving directly from Europe increased. New Englanders moved into eastern and northern Ohio, which also received many people from Pennsylvania and New Jersey. The largest number of pioneers in the Old Northwest in this period came, however, from the South, especially from Virginia and North Carolina. Some, who were pioneers or sons of pioneers in Kentucky and Tennessee, were on the move again, feeling that the large planters were already squeezing them out.

The pioneers' movement, day after day, by land and water, was an awesome sight, as many observers commented. One wrote: "Old America seems to be breaking up, and moving westward. We are seldom out of sight, as we travel on this grand track toward the Ohio, of family groups, behind and before us." One farmer in upstate New York, in nine days, counted 260 wagons on their way to Ohio. Three thousand families gathered at Olean, New York, in the spring of 1818, to wait for the thaw so they could float down the Allegheny River to Pittsburgh and then on down the Ohio. Families used the river flatboats as houseboats, complete with living quarters and livestock.

Between Georgia and the Mississippi lay a smaller frontier area than the Old Northwest. Out of this Old Southwest were formed the states of Alabama and Mississippi. Here land buying and speculation were more spectacular than in the northern area. The soil of the gulf plains was the best then found for growing cotton, so by

1819 sales were at the rate of 2,278,000 acres a year and the best land was selling for $30 an acre. Half the nation's cotton grew here and the population was 200,000.

The trans-Appalachian west had its folk heroes—the men who were first into the wilderness, who fought hard and talked big, and who moved on again when such prosaic people as farmers settled in. One of these heroes was David (Davy) Crockett (1786–1836). He fought under Andrew Jackson in 1813–14 against the Creek Indians, was elected to the Tennessee legislature and later to the House of Representatives. Even then, though, he was better known for his exploits in the wilds and his tall tales than as a legislator. It is impossible to say how many of the stories about him were made up by others, but no one seemed to mind. In one nine-month period, he was said to have killed 105 bears—one by hugging it to death. He had a tame panther that brushed off the hearth every morning with its tail. He knew a man who was so ugly flies wouldn't land on his face. So the stories went. Defeated for reelection in 1835, Crockett took off for Texas where the next year he died with the other defenders of the Alamo.

Hardly had the settlement of the Old Northwest started, when the far larger expanse of the Louisiana Purchase became part of the United States. Mostly unexplored and unmapped, it was a tantalizing geographical mystery, and it kept alive the dream of a water passage across the continent. Jefferson hoped, at the very least, that the navigable headwaters of the Missouri River lay so near some river flowing westward into the Pacific, that a short overland portage would be all that would be needed to complete a water route from Pittsburgh at the start of the Ohio to the far coast of Oregon or California.

Even before the area became American property a few settlers had crossed the Mississippi and moved in. Missouri, opposite Kentucky and Tennessee, was settled early, and by 1820 farms dotted the land eighty miles up the Missouri River. Enough people moved to

Arkansas by 1819 to justify giving it territorial status. For the most part, though, the reaches of Louisiana territory were seen only by explorers, traders and trappers.

Among the first to travel westward across the whole continent from the Mississippi were two intrepid and unusually capable men, Meriwether Lewis (1774–1809) and William Clark (1770–1838). Lewis had been President Jefferson's private secretary, partly to prepare for a western expedition since Jefferson had been planning, even before the Louisiana Purchase, to send a party of explorers across the Mississippi. Jefferson was motivated by scientific curiosity as well as by considerations of governmental policy. An expedition could search out the best travel route, and also help to establish America's claim to the Oregon Territory.

Lewis, the leader of the expedition, was born in Virginia and was a captain in the army. He was healthy, courageous, and a born leader, with a smattering of knowledge about plants, animals, geography and other subjects certain to be of use on such a trip. Lewis chose Clark as his co-leader. Clark was also born in Virginia and was also an army officer—a lieutenant with the courtesy title of captain for the expedition. His observations in the field of natural history, and his journals and maps were among the most useful results of the journey.

The Lewis and Clark expedition left St. Louis on May 14, 1804. The group that went all the way consisted of about thirty people, mostly army enlisted men, and included Clark's Black slave, York. Lewis had with him his Newfoundland dog, Scammon. Although the expedition came upon Indians who had never seen white men before, it had little trouble. The Indians were usually friendly; if not, Lewis and Clark simply faced them down. By November they were far up the Missouri and set up a winter camp at Fort Mandan, named for the Mandan Indians of that area, near where Bismarck, North Dakota, was later established. On Christmas Day brandy was served to all and dancing went on much of the day even though there were no women for partners. Among the events of the trip so far, the expedition had heard from Indians a story of an area inhabited by devils who were human in form, had very large heads, and were about eighteen inches tall. Another day, Lewis estimated he had seen 3,000 buffalo at one time.

In the spring Lewis and Clark and their company set out again, and on April 26, 1805, they were the first white men to see the Yellowstone River where it flows into the Missouri. They reached the Great Falls of the Missouri in June and on July 25, they came to the Three Forks, in southern Montana, where the Missouri is formed. Lewis and Clark loyally named the three rivers the Jefferson, the Madison and the Gallatin. They had now traversed almost 2,500 miles up the Missouri, a river longer than the Mississippi. As they pressed on, over rough territory, they were disappointed to find that here at least there was no short, easy passage from the Missouri to a westward-flowing river. On August 12, Lewis and a small party found a stream flowing west. They had crossed the Continental Divide. They were the first Americans to do so and the first white people between New Mexico in Spanish territory and Alberta in Canada.

From then until mid-October they experienced their roughest traveling in getting through the mountains. At that time they found the junction of the Snake and Columbia rivers in Washington, and went down the Columbia to the coast, which they reached on November 7. They hoped a ship from the East coast would meet them with supplies but none did. The expedition built its winter quarters, named Fort Clatsop for an Indian tribe, in December. For Christmas Day, 1805, Clark noted in his diary:

> We would have spent this day, the nativity of Christ, in feasting, had we had anything either to raise our spirits or even gratify our appetites. Our dinner consisted of poor elk, so much spoiled that we ate it through mere necessity, some spoiled pounded fish, and a few roots.

Early in the new year, Lewis in his diary recorded:

> Our party, from necessity having been obliged to subsist some length of time on dogs, have now become extremely fond of their flesh.

The party must have been happy to start back east on March 23, 1806. The leaders split up at one time, in the area of the Yellowstone River, then rejoined. The journey back was much as before, except that with the knowledge they had gained it was less difficult. Finally, on September 23, after two years and four months, the Lewis and Clark expedition arrived back in St. Louis. The party suffered only three losses in all that time, in spite of hardships, wild animals, threatening Indians and illnesses. One man deserted, one private was discharged for insubordination and one man died from appendicitis.

The expedition was a tremendous triumph. It brought back great quantities of information about vegetation, animals, the Indians and the geography of the land. The leaders were disappointed that no simple land or water passage connected the West and the East, but the expedition did show that the nation was not getting too big, that men could conquer it. It was not quite true, as Theodore Roosevelt wrote near the end of the century, that "as they journeyed upstream through the bright summer weather, though they worked hard, it was work of a kind which was but a long holiday." It was true, though, as he also wrote in *The Winning of the West,* that

> they had done a great deed, for they had opened the door into the heart of the far West. Close on their tracks followed the hunters, trappers, and fur traders who themselves made ready the way for the settlers whose descendants were to possess the land.

Lewis became governor of Louisiana Territory in 1807. While on his way to Washington two years later, he died by violence at a lonely inn in Tennessee. Whether it was murder or suicide no one has ever been able to say. Clark was named superintendent of Indian affairs in 1807, then fought in the War of 1812. He was governor of Missouri Territory from 1813 to 1821 when he resumed his Indian affairs post, which he held until his death.

Those who have written about the Lewis and Clark expedition have been fascinated by the one woman who took part in it—Sacajawea, a Snake Indian who was called Bird Woman. In her teens she was captured by another tribe, then when she was about eighteen, she was taken by a French-Canadian, Tousaint Charbonneau, as his second wife. At Fort Mandan, in the winter of 1804–05, Sacajawea and her husband joined the expedition as guides and interpreters. She bore a son in February, 1805, and the baby accompanied the expedition to the coast and back. This helped to show Indians along the way that the expedition was not a war party. Some of the land was familiar to Sacajawea, and she was the only one able to deal satisfactorily with the Shoshone Indians when the party met them in the summer of 1805.

She fell ill once during the journey, but Lewis and Clark nursed her back to health. When the baby became sick, Clark noted in his diary that they applied "a poultice of onions, after giving him some cream of tartar." Sacajawea left the expedition when it returned to the Mandan country. After she died in 1812, Clark became the guardian of the boy and of another child she had borne. Sacajawea's character and common sense made her a memorable woman. Many statues have been erected in her honor.

Even before Lewis and Clark returned, other exploring parties were penetrating the unknown West. Zebulon Pike (1779–1813), a professional army officer, was sent in 1805 to find the source of the Mississippi River. He thought he had succeeded, but was mistaken. In 1806–07 he led an expedition in the southwest, going up the Arkansas River to the site of Pueblo, Colorado. On this trip he discovered the mountain later named for him, Pikes Peak, although he did not climb it. He estimated its height at 18,000 feet, which was 4,000 feet too much. On the return part of his journey, he entered Spanish territory and was taken prisoner by the Spaniards. After some time, he was allowed to return to the United States. A few people thought he was involved with the plans and plots of Burr and Wilkinson, but he was exonerated and continued an honorable career.

Stephen Long (1784–1864), of the Corps of Engineers, was another army professional who increased the nation's knowledge of its western lands. He explored the upper Mississippi in 1817 and in 1819–20 he led a party into the Rockies, camping on the present site of the city of Denver. He discovered Longs Peak, named for him, and became the first white man to climb Pikes Peak. Finally, in 1823, he led an expedition to seek the source of the Minnesota River and to study the United States–Canadian boundary. In his 1819–20 expedition, Long's party included two artists. As time went on, more and more artists joined in the exploration of the West, leaving a valuable record of the country as it was in the nineteenth century. Samuel Seymour (1797–1882) did watercolors of such scenes as "Kiowa Encampment" and "Pawnee Council." Titian Ramsay Peale (1799–1885) also did watercolors of animals and Indian villages, including "Sioux Lodge."

Along with their valuable fact-finding journeys, Pike and Long also fostered the myth of a "Great American Desert," a term they applied to the High Plains region east of the Rockies, extending as far as central Nebraska. Pike believed that "these vast plains of the western hemisphere may become in time equally celebrated with the sandy deserts of Africa." Long agreed: "I do not hesitate in giving the opinion, that it is almost wholly unfit for cultivation, and of course, uninhabitable by a people depending upon agriculture for their subsistence." This myth was not dispelled until the middle of the century, when the area was recognized for what it was: not a lush paradise but a region where certain kinds of agriculture and grazing could be sustained.

The trans-Mississippi west attracted the interest of scientists, too. Thomas Nuttal (1786–1859), director of the Harvard botanical garden, made several trips through the West and wrote a book about his experiences. As a paleontologist he was interested in discovering the remains of extinct forms of life in the region.

Until the Adams-Onís Treaty of 1819, the southwestern boundary of the Louisiana Purchase was vague and some Americans wanted to claim all of Texas. Jefferson had some exploration carried out along the boundary of Texas, using William Dunbar (1749–1810) as his agent. Scottish-born Dunbar was a scientist and a Mississippi planter. His meteorological observations in the Natchez region led to a correspondence with Jefferson. In 1804 he explored the Ouachita River country in Arkansas, and two years later the Red River along the northern boundary of Texas. His record of the mineral springs at Hot Springs, Arkansas, is the first note of their existence.

Although the United States renounced any claim to Texas, the planters of the South had their eyes on its fertile acres. Somewhat surprisingly, first the Spaniards, and then the independent Mexican government after the revolution of 1821, encouraged American settlers. Spanish authorities were usually suspicious of the motives of Americans who entered their lands. Moses Austin (1761–1821) received a grant of land and permission to bring in 300 settlers in 1820. The Mexican government confirmed this the following year, but Austin died before he could take advantage of it. His son, Stephen Fuller Austin (1793–1836), took up the grant and in 1822 led the first large group of Americans to settle legally in Texas. Mexico further encouraged American settlement in 1823, when the government offered a square league (about nine square miles) to pioneers at 12.5 cents an acre.

Further into the southwest than Texas lay New Mexico and its one city, Santa Fe. American traders were interested in it as a place where a great deal of business could be done, but until Mexican independence the Spaniards kept it closed to outsiders. After 1821, however, an annual flow of men and goods reached Santa Fe from Missouri, and the Santa Fe Trail became an important line of communication into the southwest. The Americans took textiles and hardware to Santa Fe in caravans that consisted of as many as a hundred wagons.

The fur trade was the most lucrative occupation in the unsettled parts of the North American continent. When the French held Canada and the Mississippi Valley, the exploits of their trappers in the wilds were widely known. After the British received title to Canada in 1763, they also encouraged trapping, chiefly through the Hudson's Bay Company. Even after the American Revolution, the British tried to hold onto the fur trade in the Old Northwest. They were now active west of the Mississippi, notably in Oregon territory. One of the first activities of Americans once Louisiana was theirs was to go after furs in the northwest.

The fur trade required adventurous men who were willing to go off alone into unknown country to seek valuable furs, mostly beaver. The business also required men with capital and organizational skill to finance the trapping and to provide a market for the furs. One of these early entrepreneurs was Manuel Lisa (1772–1820) who by 1800 was well-established at St. Louis and had a monopoly of fur trading with the Osage Indians. Encouraged by the reports of the Lewis and Clark expedition, he sent several exploring and trapping parties up the Missouri and one up the Yellowstone. In 1809 Lisa joined with the Chouteau family to found the Missouri Fur Company.

The Chouteaus came originally from New Orleans and developed their family business into one of the most extensive trading organizations in the West. René Auguste Chouteau (1749–1829), when only fourteen years old, accompanied an expedition to found a trading post, and the site the party chose in 1764 became the city of St. Louis. He was skillful in dealing with Indian tribes and after the War of 1812 the government sought his aid in negotiating treaties with them. When St. Louis was incorporated in 1809, René Auguste was the first chairman of the trustees. His brother, Jean Pierre (1758–1849), was active in the firm and established a trading post on the site of Salina, Oklahoma.

The firm prospered even more under Jean Pierre's two sons, Auguste Pierre (1786–1838) and Pierre (1789–1865). Auguste Pierre was a West Point graduate. On an expedition along the upper Arkansas River in 1817, he was captured by the Spanish and held prisoner at Santa Fe for several months. Pierre became the most successful of the family, branching out with his own company whose mercantile operations went far beyond the fur trade, making him one of the wealthiest of western financiers.

William Henry Ashley (1778–1838) also operated out of St. Louis. Besides managing a successful business, he contributed considerably to the exploration of the West and to establishing American claims to disputed territory. His first expedition in 1822 built a post at the mouth of the Yellowstone. The next year an Ashley expedition in the upper Missouri had to turn back because of the hostility of the Arikaras Indians. He was with a party in 1825 that crossed from the upper Platte River to the Green River valley to explore it for the first time. Ashley's innovation in fur trading was to substitute an annual rendezvous for the fixed trading posts. Once a year he would set a site for a rendezvous and, when the appointed time came, the trappers would gather there to sell their furs and to purchase supplies. This system was more flexible as the rendezvous location could be changed as conditions changed. The rendezvous was a necessity for the trapper, but often his first taste of civilization in a year was too much for him, and most of what he received for his furs went for drinks and gambling before he headed for the trapping country once more.

The fur trade played a central part in building the first of the large American fortunes, that of John Jacob Astor (1763–1848). Born in Germany, Astor arrived in the United States in 1784 without a cent to his name. Before many years he made a great deal of money out of the trade with China and was investing shrewdly in New York real estate. Astor formed the American Fur Company in 1808 to compete with the British-Canadian Hudson's Bay Company and the North West Company. As part of his farflung operations, Astor established the trading post of Astoria near the mouth of the Columbia River in Oregon in 1811. A year later, however, when war broke out with Great Britain, Astor sold it to the British North West Company rather than simply abandon it. Astoria was restored to the United States in 1818. Even though driven out of Oregon at this time, the activities of the American Fur Company helped establish America's claim to the area.

Astor also carried out fur-trading operations in the Great Lakes region, although this business was damaged by the war, too. After the war foreign traders were excluded from the United States and in 1821 Astor allied himself with the Chouteau interests. The two enterprises together secured a practical monopoly on the fur trade in the Missouri Valley and the Rocky Mountains. The Astor-Chouteau combination bought out competitors, or otherwise tried to put them out of business by its superior trading and financial power, making the operation one of the first monopolies in the country.

One of Astor's men, Robert Stuart (1785–1843), discovered a pass that later took on historical importance in the settlement of the West. Stuart, who was born in Scotland, went to Canada in 1807, became a fur trader and joined Astor's Astoria venture. Leading a party east in 1812, he and his group became the first white people known to have used the South Pass. This Rocky Mountain pass, in southwestern Wyoming, is a broad level valley at an altitude of about 7,500 feet. It was later an important point on the Oregon Trail and thousands of emigrant wagons were driven through it.

The men who organized the fur trade—and made money out of it—were necessary, and some went on expeditions themselves. The backbone of the fur trade, though, consisted of the "mountain men" who spent most of their lives in the wilderness, seeking the valuable beaver skins. Some of these men formed their own companies or groups, but for the most part they were a breed of individualists. They flourished only in the 1820's to the 1840's and there were probably no more than 600 of them in all. Nevertheless, they have entered history as folk heroes and as the advance guard of the nation that conquered the West, especially in the High Plains and the Rocky Mountains.

They had to be hardy and self-reliant, with the skills to survive alone in inhospitable country. They sometimes lived with the Indians, and at least had to be able to get along with them. Sometimes they were traders, guides or interpreters as well as trappers and, indirectly, they added a great deal to the store of geographical knowledge of the trans-Mississippi west. The mountain men chose this life for adventure and excitement, perhaps to escape eastern law, as well as a way to make a living. The average life span does not appear to have been very long.

They had a well-deserved reputation for being rough and tough. An English traveler set down his impressions:

> . . . their habits and character assume a most singular cast of simplicity mingled with ferocity. . . . Keen observers of nature, they rival the beasts of prey in discovering the haunts and habits of game, and in their skill and cunning in capturing it. Constantly exposed to perils of all kinds, they become callous to any feeling of danger, and destroy human as well as animal life with as little scruple and as freely as they expose their own. . . . I *have* met honest moun-

tain-men. . . . these alone are the hardy pioneers who have paved
the way for the settlement of the western country.

The same observer also gave a vivid picture of what a mountain man
looked like:

> The costume of the trapper is a hunting-shirt of dressed buckskin,
> ornamented with long fringes; pantaloons of the same material, and
> decorated with porcupine quills and long fringes down the outside
> of the leg. A flexible felt hat and moccasins clothe his extremities.
> Over his left shoulder and under his right arm hang his powder-
> horn and bullet-pouch, in which he carries his balls, flint and steel,
> and odds and ends of all kinds. Round the waist is a belt, in which
> is stuck a large butcher-knife in a sheath of buffalo-hide, made fast
> to the belt by a chain or guard of steel . . . . A tomahawk is also
> often added; and, of course, a long heavy rifle is part and parcel of
> his equipment.

Any account of the mountain men and their exploits cannot
overlook John Colter (1775–1813), who was born in Virginia, enlisted
in the Lewis and Clark expedition in 1803, and in 1807 acted as a
guide for Manuel Lisa. Sent out to find the Blackfoot Indians in
order to trade with them, he traveled alone through some of the
roughest, unknown country in the West. He crossed the Continental
Divide and passed through some of the future Yellowstone Park.
Having met some Crow Indians, he fought with them against the
Blackfeet. A year or so later the Blackfeet, seeking revenge, captured
him and killed his partner. He escaped, naked and barefoot, hid in
water for a whole day and then traveled seven days before he reached
safety.

James Bridger (1804–81) was also born in Virginia. He joined
Ashley's 1822 expedition. From then on he was one of the best-known
traders and trappers. Although illiterate, he knew a number of Indian
languages and was invaluable as an interpreter. He was probably the
first white person to see Great Salt Lake, in 1825. Later he founded
Fort Bridger on the Oregon Trail.

Thomas Fitzpatrick (c. 1799–1854), from Ireland, also participated in Ashley expeditions. He later became the senior partner in
the Rocky Mountain Fur Company and in 1842 guided the first emigrant wagon train to Oregon. His Indian name was "Broken Hand."

Jedediah Strong Smith (1799–1831) was perhaps the outstanding
mountain man of them all. He was born in New York State and had
his first western experience with Ashley. He stood out even then, a
six-foot tall, Bible-reading young man who was an excellent marks-
man. He and Fitzpatrick took a party through the South Pass early
in 1824 and inaugurated its regular use, although Stuart had found
it a dozen years before. His most notable adventure was a trip that
began in 1825. With a small party, he traveled southwest from Great
Salt Lake, across the Colorado River and the Mojave Desert, to San
Diego, California. The Spaniards there were surprised and not too
pleased to see him. Smith and two of his men headed back east, becoming, so far as is known, the first white people to cross the Sierra
Nevada (the California mountain range) and the dreaded Great Salt
Desert. Smith was killed by Comanche Indians on the Cimarron
River in 1831. More than any other person, he blazed trails that were
useful to thousands who followed after him on the way to California
and Oregon.

Mike Fink (c. 1770–c. 1823) was born in Pittsburgh. He was first
a keelboatman on the western rivers until the steamboat took over.
Going west to become a trapper, he joined Ashley's first expedition.
Somewhere near the mouth of the Yellowstone he was killed in a
brawl. Fink contributed little to the exploration of the West, but
much to the legends of the trappers and of the river boatmen who
enjoyed a reputation for being even tougher and meaner than the
mountain men. Fink is remembered more for the tall tales about his
exploits than anything else.

Hugh Glass was a mountain man from about 1822 to 1833. He
is remembered chiefly because of his experience when he was mauled

by a grizzly bear and left for dead by his companions. He came to and dragged himself a hundred miles to Fort Kiowa. He recovered, only to be killed later by Indians.

A panoramic view of the United States between 1800 and 1825 shows a steady progression from east to west of the three stages of the frontier. At the start of the century, explorers and trappers were only beginning to venture into the great plains and mountains west of the Mississippi. On the other side of the river and eastward to the Appalachians, the supremacy of the hunter and trapper was starting to pass. Farmers and town builders were breaking soil and putting up buildings. By 1825, the settling process was continuing west of the Mississippi, while in the East the frontier was mostly gone and the farms, houses and towns were beginning to look much like those in the original Atlantic coast area. The process kept repeating itself onward to the Pacific coast.

For trapper or for settler, the West did not offer an easy life. The trappers' lives were considered more glamorous and exciting, and their exploits have been recorded more often than those, for example, of a young farmer and his family who left New England for the Illinois country. But clearing land, building a log cabin or house, keeping a family from starving until crops could be counted on was also hard—on the nerves as well as on the muscles. And, as the historian Henry Adams wrote in 1889 when memories of pioneer days were nearer at hand:

> . . . whatever trials the men endured, the burden bore most heavily upon the women and children. The chance of being shot or scalped by Indians was hardly worth considering when compared with the certainty of malarial fever, or the strange disease called milk-sickness, or the still more depressing home-sickness, or the misery of nervous prostration, which wore out generation after generation of women and children on the frontiers, and left tragedy in every log-cabin. Not for love of ease did men plunge into the wilderness.

9 Indians and Whites

AMERICAN INDIANS and African Blacks had much in common in 1800. Both were more at the mercy of white people than in earlier years, and their situations were getting worse. White settlers were pushing the Indians off fertile land east of the Mississippi and herding them westward. And every year other whites were bringing thousands of African Blacks into the southeast to work as slaves, in some instances on land from which the Indians were being moved. White superiority in attitude and in power made inferior beings of both Indians and Blacks.

The Indians in 1800 were still a definite physical menace on the frontier, and they took many scalps from among the settlers—who were inclined to see them only as savages with no rights. As a result of treaties and warfare, along with the relentless tide of frontiersmen, the Indian menace east of the Mississippi was over by the end of the quarter century. When the danger from the Indians lessened, the people of the United States and their government were left with a moral problem: how to deal with a people whose way of life they had shattered. President Jefferson was of two minds about the Indians. He felt an obligation to see that they were justly treated and he hoped they would settle down as farmers, thus ending the danger of blood-shed and requiring less land than they did in a nomadic way of life. At the same time, he wanted to move as many Indians as possible away from the nation's borders, so that they would not be a threat if Great Britain or France had occasion to arouse them against the Americans.

The physical danger from the Indians east of the Mississippi was greatly eased in 1815 with the conclusion of the war and the final withdrawal of British influence in the Old Northwest. President Monroe in 1817 proposed that grants of land be made to the eastern Indians, who had by now given up much of the territory they once claimed. "It is our duty," he said, "to make new efforts for the preservation, improvement and civilization of the native inhabitants." Most people in the western part of the country disagreed. They wanted all the Indians forced across the Mississippi, and before Monroe left office an Indian Territory was established there for tribes that could be induced to leave the East.

Indian culture as well as Indian land was under pressure from the white man. As their way of life became more constricted, the Indians became more dependent on the government, or its agents, for guns and tools—and for the whiskey that hastened their demoralization. In 1795 Congress established a system of trading with the Indians that lasted until 1822. Under the direction of the War Department—which for better or for worse had more dealings with the Indians than any other department—trading houses, called factories, were established where the Indians could trade furs for merchandise. Some private individuals were also licensed to carry on this trade. The purpose was to protect the Indians from being cheated and to supply them with goods at low prices. Business interests, such as those of John Jacob Astor, agitated for the government to get out of business and stop "competing" with private firms, which it did in 1822.

A move to "civilize" the Indians by integrating them into the white way of life began in 1819 with the passage of an act to educate at least some of them. An annual appropriation of $10,000 was provided, which limited the scope of the program. Thirty-two schools were in operation in 1824, with 916 children attending. The conflicting policies of educating the Indians on the one hand while seizing their land and harassing them westward on the other are reflected in the debate over the basic character of the Indians. Were they physically and mentally inferior, or were they the victims of their environment?

Jefferson believed the Indians were savages, but that this was caused by their environment. They could be civilized through education. Henry Clay did not believe they could be civilized and that as an inferior race they were doomed to extinction. Yet Clay had a good record of defending the rights of the Indians.

One of the first to try to take an objective view of Indian culture by studying it scientifically was Henry Rowe Schoolcraft (1793–1864), a self-taught ethnologist who made several explorations to study Indian culture. He accompanied an expedition to the upper Mississippi and Lake Superior region in 1820, and two years later he was appointed Indian agent for the tribes in that area. Here Schoolcraft carried on his ethnological studies for nearly twenty years and married an Ojibwa woman, the daughter of a fur trader.

From the time the United States was established, treaties were frequently negotiated with Indian tribes east of the Mississippi. By agreement, guile or threat, the Indians were induced to sign away millions of acres of land. In return they received, chiefly, promises which were usually broken. A leading negotiator of treaties in the Old Northwest was William Henry Harrison (1773–1841), who was appointed governor of Indiana Territory when he was twenty-seven and held the post from 1800 to 1812. In that time he signed fifteen treaties with the Indians. Harrison faithfully carried out government policy, and was as anxious as anyone to clear title to the potential farmlands in his territory so that white settlers could move in. He was not blind, however, to the crimes committed by his fellow citizens. He noted how they encroached on Indian lands in defiance of the law. White juries, Harrison observed, were quick to hang an Indian who murdered a white man, but no white man was ever convicted of killing an Indian.

One treaty, signed in 1804 and of doubtful validity, had repercussions as late as the 1830's. By the original treaty, the Sac and Fox Indians agreed to give up their land in the Illinois area and to move across the Mississippi, but they were not required to do this until the tide of frontier settlement reached them. One chief, Black Hawk (1767–1838), who fought for the British in the War of 1812, opposed the treaty and as a result, skirmishes with the whites went on for years. Black Hawk did not have the support of another chief, Keokuk (1780–1848), who favored the United States in the war and who was willing to sell tribal lands. Keokuk was a popular leader and an excellent orator who used his talents later in arguing for his people in Washington. The struggle with Black Hawk culminated in enough military action to be named the Black Hawk War in 1832. Abraham Lincoln served briefly in one of the militia units sent to fight the Indians.

By the Treaty of Fort Wayne, in September, 1809, Harrison secured almost 3,000,000 acres of land, running for nearly a hundred miles on each side of the Wabash River. A number of tribes were involved in the deal. This, and other treaties, were protested by Tecumseh (1768–1813), chief of the Shawnees. He contended that no one tribe had the right to turn over land to the Americans and that action should be taken jointly by all tribes. To Governor Harrison he said:

> Once, there was not a white man in all this country. Then, it all belonged to the redmen; children of the same parents—placed on it by the Great Spirit, to keep it, to travel over it, to eat its fruits, and fill it with the same race.

Harrison was disturbed by Tecumseh's activities, but he agreed that Tecumseh was "one of those uncommon geniuses which spring up occasionally to produce revolutions and overturn the established order of things."

Tecumseh was aided by his brother, the Shawnee Prophet (1775?–1837?) who claimed he had received a message from the spirit world that all Indians should renounce the ways of the white man and return to their old and entirely Indian way of life. His influence was great, aided no little when he foretold a solar eclipse in 1806. Tecumseh traveled all over his midwest area and into the South, trying to unite the many tribes. While he was away in late 1811, Harrison marched his troops into Indian land near the Prophet's village on the Tippecanoe River in Indiana. The Indians attacked early on the morning of November 11, and nearly broke the American forces. In the end, the battle was somewhat of a standoff, but the military power of the Shawnees was shattered. Thirty years later this battle helped Harrison win election as president of the United States with the slogan "Tippecanoe and Tyler Too." Harrison won but died within a month of taking office in 1841, and Vice-President John Tyler succeeded him.

The signing of treaties and the moving of Indians to make way for white settlers went on. Treaties in 1818–19 secured further large tracts of land in Indiana and Illinois from tribes who were moved out of the area. By 1824, 8,000 such Indians had been shifted to southwestern Missouri. Even then more than 12,000 Indians remained in parts of Ohio, Michigan, Indiana and Illinois. So many treaties for ceding land were signed that one investigator found fifty-four acts transferring land, many of them overlapping, in the one state of Indiana. One of the 1819 treaties was with the Kickapoo Indians. They aided Tecumseh during the War of 1812 when he fought for the British, and later helped the Sac and Fox in the Black Hawk War. After that the Kickapoo were forced to go to Missouri. The Ojibwa

Indians in the middle of the eighteenth century were one of the largest tribes, numbering about 25,000 and controlling land in the Lake Superior-Lake Huron region. They, too, fought for the British in the war, but later signed a peace treaty with the United States and settled down on reservations. Other tribes in the Old Northwest had similar experiences and slowly but surely had to give in to the never-ending pressure of the Americans entering their lands.

In the southeast the leading Indian tribes were the Cherokee, the Creek and the Seminole, and of these the Cherokee tribe was the largest and most important. The whites considered the Cherokees superior to other Indians, because they came nearer to meeting the standards of American civilization. They set up a governmental system in 1820 patterned after that of the United States. They welcomed white people and established such institutions as churches and schools. As the Cherokees settled down to farming, they increased in population and one group moved across the Mississippi. A census in 1825 showed more than 13,000 of them in the East. Among them were 147 white men and 73 white women who had married Cherokee mates. The tribe owned 1,277 Black slaves. The Cherokee Nation was a going enterprise, producing cotton and wool, but the greedier whites of Georgia wanted their land. The Cherokees fought a civilized battle in the courts, but lawless whites defied the courts and drove the Indians from their farms.

Sequoyah (c. 1770–1843) was the Cherokee who brought literacy to his people. The son of a white trader and a Cherokee woman, he was also known as George Guess. He was a silversmith, among other things, but his chief occupation became that of devising an alphabet for the Cherokee language. He succeeded, using a syllabary of eighty-five characters. He demonstrated its utility by having his twelve-year-old daughter take down what was said at a tribal council while he remained outside. He then entered and read off the speeches from his daughter's writing. He traveled widely to spread his alphabet and the Cherokee became a literate Indian nation. Parts of the Bible were printed in Cherokee and in 1828 a newspaper was established. The giant sequoia tree is named for Sequoyah.

The Creek Indians of Alabama and Georgia rebelled against the United States during the War of 1812 and were badly defeated by General Jackson. They were an agricultural people and had settled fifty towns, or tribal groups, which joined in a confederation—chiefly for protection against other Indians to the north. William MacIntosh (c. 1775–1825) was the son of a British army officer and a Creek woman. He was friendly to the Americans, was made a brigadier general in the war and fought with Jackson against the Seminoles. With some of the Creek chiefs, MacIntosh signed a treaty in 1825 ceding the remaining 10,000,000 acres of Creek land to Georgia. He had no right to do this, since only the whole Creek nation in council could decide such a matter. He was sentenced to death by the council, and the sentence was carried out by a party of Creek warriors.

The Seminole Indians separated from the Creeks in the early eighteenth century and settled in Florida. They absorbed other Indians from farther north and also many runaway slaves. They were the target of General Jackson's 1817–18 armed expedition into Florida. Beginning in 1835 the Seminoles fought the longest and costliest of any Indian war against the United States Army. Eventually the Seminoles—along with the Cherokees and Creeks, as well as two other southeastern tribes, the Choctaw and the Chickasaw—were moved to Oklahoma where they became known as the "Five Civilized Tribes."

While the Indians east of the Mississippi were being cajoled or forced into ceding their lands, and pressured to move across the river, most of the Indians in the area of the Louisiana Purchase were meeting the white man for the first time. Before this period, they had at most been in contact with a few traders and trappers. Later the pressure on the Indians of the West to hand over their lands to the whites and to settle on reservations was to become as great as it already was in the East. In the early nineteenth century, however, they were, for the most part, still living as they had for generations.

The western Indians that the white explorers and traders were meeting were divided into two basic types. On the eastern Great Plains, toward the Mississippi, the Indians were semi-agricultural, made up mostly of the Sioux (or Dakota) Indians, who were the dominant group of many related tribes. They were strong as far south as Louisiana. In dress and other styles, these semi-agricultural peoples were partly like the Indians in the East, but they also followed some of the customs of the Indians farther west. Their clothing was made from skins, was quite elaborate and was decorated with quills. After the white man came they used beads for decoration. The men of different tribes favored different hair styles. Some shaved their heads, leaving only center strips. The men also wore feathered headdresses as symbols of their prowess in combat. The people lived in villages and many tribes built earth-covered lodges.

A somewhat different way of life prevailed farther west and has provided the standard image of the western Indian, mounted on a horse, hunting buffalo, or attacking emigrant wagon trains. Non-agricultural, they depended mostly on buffalo-hunting, together with digging up roots and picking berries, for their food. They lived in portable tipis—conical-shaped tents that were covered with buffalo hides. The men wore breechcloths and moccasins; in cold weather they put on more clothes and used buffalo robes for warmth. Women wore sleeveless leather dresses and moccasins. Like their neighbors to the east, the men wore headdresses, including the distinctive war bonnets with trailing feathers.

The Hidatsa, Mandan and Crow Indians were all of Siouan stock. There were about 2,000 Hidatsa when Lewis and Clark came upon them in 1804, but later smallpox, one of the white people's diseases that did as much as anything else to weaken Indian power, sharply reduced their numbers. They and the Mandans (near whom Lewis and Clark spent their first winter) were village dwellers. Their villages were palisaded and were often located on bluffs overlooking the Missouri River. Their dwellings were mound-shaped and the villages were trading centers. The Mandans contributed to one of the favorite myths about the New World. When they were first encountered, there were a few individuals with pale skin and light-colored hair among them. From this came the story that they were the long-lost descendants of Welshmen. These Welshmen supposedly had accompanied the Welsh Prince Madoc who, according to legend, discovered America 300 years before Columbus. The Crow Indians were a hunting tribe in the Yellowstone River area. Although related to the Sioux, they were their enemies and helped the whites in war with them.

The Pawnee Indians in Kansas and Nebraska were visited by General Pike on his expedition. They were distinguished by their mythology and ritualism, which was much more elaborate than most Indian religious practices. The Pawnees were a warlike people but they never fought against the United States, even when they were badly treated. The Arikara Indians, related to the Pawnees, were builders of substantial homes and villages. They were friendly toward Lewis and Clark but later were in conflict with the whites. A treaty with them was signed in 1825, ending the difficulty. Still farther into the northwest were the Nez Percé, who occupied a large area in Idaho, Oregon and Washington. The French gave them their name because some of the Nez Percé wore pendants in their noses. They lived by fishing for salmon and by gathering roots. After the horse was introduced in about 1700, they became skillful breeders of the animals. Lewis and Clark visited the Nez Percé on their way to the West coast. The Klikitat Indians numbered no more than about 700 when Lewis and Clark saw them in 1805, but from their location in south-central Washington they acted as middlemen between the tribes of the Pacific coast and those of the interior.

Back on the Atlantic coast side of the mountains, the "Indian problem" had been "solved" for some time. In fact, some of those who were most horrified by what troops and settlers in the Old Northwest and elsewhere were doing to the Indians were the New Englanders whose ancestors had solved the problem the same way a hundred years earlier by killing and scattering the Indians in their areas. Those Indians left in the East were now docile, often degraded, and living mostly on reservations, a preview of what was to come in the West.

A few leaders among the eastern Indians were still alive and were remembered for past exploits. Cornplanter (c. 1740–1836) was a Seneca chief (the Senecas were part of the once powerful Iroquois confederacy of Five Nations in New York State) who fought for the British in the American Revolution. Later he became friendly toward the whites. Cornplanter was granted land on the Allegheny River where, since the date of his birth is uncertain, he lived until he may well have been over a hundred years old.

Red Jacket (c. 1758–1830) was another Seneca chief. His name came from a bright red jacket the British gave him when he supported them in the Revolution. Later he joined Cornplanter in advocating peace with the United States. Cornplanter always considered Red Jacket a coward when it came to actual warfare, although he fought in the American army in the War of 1812. Red Jacket was a noted orator and very proud of his ability. On his deathbed, he said boastfully that when he died the whole world would say: "Red Jacket the great orator is dead."

Handsome Lake (c. 1735–1815), a Seneca religious prophet, was a half brother of Cornplanter. After an illness in 1800, he had visions and began to preach a new religion which he said had been revealed to him. His teachings were somewhat like Christian ethics and had a deep and lasting effect on the Senecas and other Iroquois. Missionaries who wanted to Christianize the Indians did not like Handsome Lake's success. He hoped the Indians would give up their old ways and become good farmers, an idea which Red Jacket made clear he hated.

Painters were attracted to the Indians, perhaps feeling the need to capture Indian life and dress before they disappeared. Red Jacket was a favorite subject. The War Department established an Indian gallery in Washington, D.C., where from 1821 to 1838 Charles Bird King (1785–1862) painted portraits of chiefs who came to visit "The Great White Father" in the White House. Sometimes King was so busy he had to have an assistant. More than a hundred portraits were completed for a three-volume work on Indian tribes. Included were fifteen Plains Indians who came all the way from across the Mississippi.

In the days of warfare between the Indians and the settlers, the Indians often took women and children captive, and many of them then spent the rest of their lives with their captors. The best known of these was Mary Jemison (1743–1833), who later was called "The White Woman of the Genesee." She was born during her parents' voyage to America from Ireland. Captured in 1758, during the French and Indian Wars, she was adopted by the Senecas. She was later twice married—once to a Delaware and once to a Seneca—and had eight children, always refusing to leave the Senecas even when she could. In 1817 New York State confirmed her possession of land along the Genesee River, which had been given her in 1797.

A bird's-eye view of the Indian-white relationship in the first quarter of the century reveals a repeated pattern which moved remorselessly from East to West. When there was no longer an Indian problem east of the Appalachians, the bloodiest part of the process was being acted out between the Appalachians and the Mississippi. West of the Mississippi, at the same time, first contacts were being made, as they had been two-hundred years before, on the Atlantic coast. It was not hard to predict what would happen next on the Great Plains.

WHEN THE UNITED STATES achieved independence in the 1780's, slavery was almost universal in the thirteen states. Some of the leading Founding Fathers wanted to take the occasion of organizing the Federal government to end slavery, but when they found they could not do this and have union too, they abandoned their antislavery position in favor of a nation that would include all the former colonies. Many persons at the time, including Southerners, viewed slavery as something that would not continue indefinitely. There was, however, neither any great movement to get rid of it, nor any very clear thinking as to how emancipation might be brought about.

By the early 1800's the picture had already changed. Slavery had disappeared in the North, where there was some moral sentiment against it and little reason to defend it since it was of no economic importance. The New England states were among the first to abolish slavery, although their merchants and shipowners continued to profit by transporting slaves from Africa to the American South. New Jersey ended slavery in 1804, the last northern state to do so, while the law organizing the Old Northwest forbade slavery there.

On the other hand, slavery was growing in the South, and more rapidly than had been expected. One stimulus, already mentioned, was the invention of the cotton gin. More slaves were needed to produce the increasing amount of cotton demanded by the textile industry in the United States and Great Britain. In addition, and especially after the War of 1812, southern slaveholders and cotton growing were both moving west. Kentucky and Tennessee, even before the war, were settled mostly by southern emigrants, while Alabama and Mississippi were ideal for cotton growing. Louisiana, in the area around New Orleans, was already slave territory when added to the union by purchase in 1803.

The official census figures show how, year by year, slavery was fastening itself and its multitude of social, economic and moral problems on the body of southern life. There were 1,002,037 Blacks in the United States in 1800, of whom not quite 900,000 were slaves. Of the slaves, 36,505 were in the northern states and the number was declining. By 1810, the Blacks numbered 1,377,808, of whom almost 1,200,000 were slaves. Another ten years and the total had risen to 1,771,656 and more than 1,500,000 of them were slaves. During this period the Blacks made up between 18 and 19 per cent of the total population. The southern slaves are usually thought of as plantation hands, but by 1820, 20 per cent of the population of the cities in the South was Black. The spread of slavery into Alabama and Mississippi can be seen in the fact that in 1810 the total population, Black and white, was 40,000, while ten years later, 75,000 slaves were at work there.

As the economic value of slavery increased, so did the arguments to justify its retention as a necessary way of life for part of the nation. It was argued, without justification, that the kind of labor required in the cotton fields could not be performed by whites—that the Negro, unlike the white, thrived under a hot sun. Another argument was even more racist: that Blacks have unique traits that make bondage a suitable and proper existence. Pseudo-scientific arguments were put forward in defense of this theory. Along the same line was the myth that Blacks were barbarians who had to be rigidly controlled for their own good, and for the protection of the white population. In effect, the defenders of slavery were saying: Now that we have these slaves, you must let us keep them that way or they will overwhelm you.

In writing the Constitution in 1787, the drafters included Article I, Section 9, which forbade Congress to prohibit: "The Migration or Importation of such persons as any of the States now existing shall think proper to admit," before 1808. In plain words, the slave traffic was safe for twenty years. As soon as the time came—in 1807—Congress passed and Jefferson signed a bill that outlawed the slave trade after January 1, 1808. The law provided for a fine of $800 for knowingly buying illegally imported slaves, and a $20,000 fine for equipping a slave ship. Great Britain abolished the slave trade in March, 1807. Violations of the law prompted Congress in 1820 to declare the traffic piracy, punishable by death, and a squadron of the navy patrolled the west coast of Africa. Nevertheless, many slaves were brought in. One estimate for 1810–20 is as high as 60,000. Perhaps a quarter of a million were imported between 1808 and 1860.

As slavery became more intricately woven into the pattern of southern life, laws—known as Black Codes—concerning slaves became stricter and more repressive. They were much the same in all the slave states, tending to be somewhat harsher in the deep South. The laws were drafted from the point of view that slaves were property, not persons. The laws, therefore, protected the owners' property rights. Provisions were also included to safeguard the whites from dangers that might arise from the large numbers of oppressed people surrounding them. The slave's duty was simply to obey a master. In Louisiana, for example, the law of 1806 stated:

> The condition of the slave being merely a passive one, his subordination to his master and to all who represent him is not susceptible of modification or restriction. . . . he owes to his master, and to all his family, a respect without bounds, and an absolute obedience. . . .

A slave had no standing in court and could not give testimony except against another slave. There were many negative restrictions: against leaving a master's land without permission; against owning firearms; against assembling in groups. Offenses against the Black Codes were punishable by whipping, branding, imprisonment or death, depending on the seriousness of the act. In practice, while a slave had little chance of being found innocent of any crime he was charged with, it was not to the self-interest of slave owners to lose the services of valuable slaves by having them shut up in prison, or executed. In some states it was difficult for an owner to free a slave even if he wanted to. An act of the state legislature might be necessary. In some states slaves could not be freed in an owner's will. Other state laws required a free slave to leave the state within a certain length of time which, of course, meant the slave had to go north. The treatment of the Blacks as a race apart was carried to such an extent that in 1810 Congress passed a law forbidding them to carry the United States mails.

While most slaves were engaged in agricultural labor, a number, especially in the southern cities, were occupied in other types of work. Some owners, in fact, hired out slaves to work in factories, on construction projects, or wherever profitable. Slaves were used in large numbers on the great plantations, but by 1860, when the slave system was at its peak, 88 per cent of all owners held fewer than twenty slaves, and most southern whites owned no slaves at all.

On the smaller farms the owner was usually his own overseer and often worked in the cotton fields along with the slaves. On the large plantations, of which the world has heard the most and whose owners wielded political influence far beyond their numbers, overseers were needed. The general rule was one slave to three acres of cotton, and an overseer for about twenty slaves. How the slaves were treated while at work depended very much on the personality of the owner. Some sought to get efficient work out of their slaves by treating them well; others believed that only the fear of punishment would make the slaves work hard. Overseers, in an unpleasant job, were the cruelest, needing both to please the owner and at the same time assert their superiority. Slave labor on the whole was not very efficient because there was no incentive for a slave to do any more work than forced to. As a result, taking it as easy as possible was common and this in turn led to frequent whippings.

Whether generous or stingy, the slave owner had a large responsibility in providing food, clothing and housing for slaves. It was to his advantage to keep them healthy, but he was also tempted to cut his costs as much as possible. Housing was simple and crude. The cabins were small, usually with no windows, certainly with no floors. Very little in the way of furniture or kitchen or sleeping equipment was provided. While these living accommodations were not as far below the standard of the log cabin of the frontier settler as they were below the standard of housing today, nevertheless they emphasized to the slave a position at the very bottom of the economic ladder.

Usually each slave family was responsible for preparing its own meals. Adult slaves received a weekly ration of three or four pounds of meat and a peck of meal. This ration was added to at times with potatoes, vegetables and fruit, while some slaves had their own vegetable gardens and chicken coops. Recreation and social life were sharply restricted, not only by slave status but also by the fact that the time and energy spent working left little opportunity for anything else. For most of the year slave life was one of unending toil, but the Christmas season was an exception. Everything except the most essential work was customarily suspended in the week between Christmas and the New Year for a period of merrymaking in which the more benevolent owners joined.

As time went on, the demand for cotton continued to increase, and the banning of the slave trade cut down the supply of fresh bodies from Africa. Thus the breeding of slaves became an industry in itself. The upper South found it was more profitable to sell surplus slaves than to expand crops in soil that was worn out. In the early years of the century, prime field hands—black males between eighteen and thirty—were worth $350 in Virginia and $500 in Louisiana. Prices kept going up so that by 1860 the going rate in Virginia was $1,000 and in Louisiana, $1,500. Slave-trading firms were established to act as middlemen between the slave breeders in the upper South and the plantation owners in the lower South. Some of these firms sold farm supplies, animals and slaves all in the same operation. Slave-trading centers were active in all the principal southern cities, including Washington, D.C., until 1850. As one historian of the American Negro puts it, many people "roundly condemned the practice of selling human beings in the capital of the world's most democratic nation."

Deliberate breeding of slaves became so established that one Virginia planter boasted his slave women were "uncommonly good breeders." Many slave girls became mothers when they were only thirteen or fourteen. In some cases a slave mother received her freedom after giving birth to ten or fifteen children. Some states had laws forbidding the breaking up of families, and in Louisiana a mother presumably could not be separated from a child under ten years of age, but such laws were seldom enforced.

The Negro slave in America was made to feel doubly degraded. Being a slave was one thing. In Greek and Roman times, white men held other white men slaves, depending on the fortunes of war. Such slaves sometimes received their freedom and rose to high positions. The African Negro, transplanted to America against his will (with the assistance of fellow Blacks in Africa), was not only a slave, but also was in an entirely alien culture under frightening circumstances. The slave was then treated, if not brutally, at best somewhat like a domestic animal. In addition to all that, it was made clear that he was inferior because of the color of his skin.

Even the most arrogant slave owner could hardly expect people living under such a burden to be happy with their lot, as much as some defenders of the institution might talk about the nobility of caring for creatures unable to look out for themselves. The South, in truth, feared the slave and the fears grew as time went on. The Black Codes contained many provisions aimed at protecting the white population. Each slave state set up a patrol system and required white men to take turns serving in it. The system was related to the militia of the state, and consisted of armed bands regularly patrolling an assigned area, especially at night, to watch out for Blacks, none of whom normally should be abroad after dark. If the patrols found Blacks who could not account for themselves, a whipping was administered on the spot.

That the South's fears were not without some basis is shown by three insurrections in the quarter century, various other incidents and any number of rumors of slave revolts. The first organized action of slaves against masters occurred in Henrico County, Virginia, in 1800, while James Monroe was governor of the state. A slave named Gabriel Prosser, from a plantation near Richmond, was the leader of about 1,000 slaves. He and his followers were betrayed by a Black, Pharaoh. Monroe called out the militia but a blow had already been struck at the conspiracy when such a heavy rain fell that the conspirators could not keep their appointed rendezvous and march on Richmond. Many slaves were arrested and thirty-five were executed. Gabriel was taken prisoner about a month later and also put to death.

More than 400 slaves in Louisiana, near New Orleans, rebelled in January, 1811. Armed with knives for cutting sugarcane, and other weapons, they killed the son of the owner of one plantation and then marched on New Orleans. Armed planters assisted by troops put the slaves to rout, killing or executing about seventy-five. The other serious and well-planned revolt of the quarter century occurred in 1822 in Charleston, South Carolina, and was led by a freed slave, Denmark Vesey (c. 1767–1822). Vesey purchased his freedom in 1800 after winning $1,500 in a lottery. He became a carpenter and through meetings in church over several years organized a plot to seize control of Charleston. He and his followers collected hundreds of weapons and enlisted the aid of a voodoo man called Gullah Jack who gave them charms against the white man's weapons. Word of the plot leaked out in June, 1822, and both the militia and federal troops were called out. Many slaves were arrested and Vesey and thirty-four others were executed. No one knew how many slaves were involved, but some estimates put the figure as high as 9,000.

Plots and rumors of plots were common throughout the period. In early 1801, less than a year after the Gabriel conspiracy, Governor Monroe received warning of another insurrection. Two slaves were seized and hanged. The North was not free from trouble even though slavery was ending there. Some Blacks in New York City in 1803 plotted to burn down the city, and did succeed in destroying eleven houses. Such activities gave slave owners an excuse for arguing that kind treatment didn't pay, and that harsh measures were needed to keep the slaves in their place. This, in turn, was an admission that the life of the slave was not one to make him content with his lot.

While sentiment for the abolition of slavery existed in both the North and the South, it was not expressed very loudly nor pursued very actively at first. After the War of 1812, however, the differences between the North and South became more apparent as the former turned to industrialism while the latter became wedded to slavery and cotton. Northern antislavery sentiment was expressed more openly after 1815, and the struggle over Missouri in 1819–20 indicated the depth and seriousness of the division that was developing.

Nevertheless, of 143 emancipation societies in the country in 1826, 103 of them were in the South. Here and there individual slave owners discarded the institution. One Virginia planter freed his slaves in 1819, took them to Illinois where he proposed to resettle and gave each family 160 acres of land. Antislavery papers and magazines were founded, such as Charles Osborn's *The Philanthropist* in 1817 in Ohio; Elihu Embree's *Emancipator* in Tennessee in 1820; and Benjamin Lundy's *Genius of Universal Emancipation* in Ohio in 1821. The "Underground Railway," a system set up by active abolitionists to smuggle slaves from the South to free territory in the North or to Canada, began operating in 1804, although it was 1831 before it was given its distinctive name.

Leading statesmen made proposals for ending slavery, usually involving reimbursement to the owners by the Federal government and the resettlement in Africa of the Blacks thus freed. In 1824, only two years before he died, Jefferson suggested such a scheme, a general idea he had also expressed many years earlier. Madison, after he left the presidency, proposed the sale of 300,000,000 acres of the public land at $2 an acre, the proceeds to be used to buy the freedom of all slaves, then numbering nearly 1,500,000. He, too, wanted to settle the Blacks in Africa.

The one practical experiment in African resettlement was carried out by the American Colonization Society, which was founded at a meeting held in Washington in December, 1816, and January, 1817. Its first plans centered on Blacks already free. President Monroe, a slaveholder, approved of the plan to acquire land in Africa and assisted the movement. Several men prominent in public life, especially Henry Clay, were active in the society's work. In 1819 Congress appropriated $100,000 to return to Africa slaves who had been illegally brought into the United States.

Land was purchased on the west coast of Africa in 1821, and the next year Liberia, the first Negro republic on the continent, was founded. Its capital was named Monrovia in 1824 in honor of President Monroe. Among the leaders who went to Liberia and helped with the actual founding were Lott Carry (1780–1828) and Jehudi Ashmun (1794–1828). Carry, a Negro Baptist missionary, sailed with the first group of twenty-eight colonists and children in 1822. He organized the First Baptist Church of Liberia and died in 1828 while defending the colony from attack. Ashmun, a Congregational minister, was sent by the Society in the early days. He found the colony in poor shape, many people ill with fever, supplies short and attack threatened by the native Africans. He and a few others reorganized affairs and successfully defended the new nation. The stricter abolitionists opposed the Society's efforts, charging that removing the free Blacks simply strengthened the grip of the South on the slaves who remained. The Blacks were not enthusiastic either. By 1860 only about 11,000 had been resettled in Liberia.

The Nashoba Community in Tennessee, founded in 1825, was another attempt to deal with the problem of slavery and the free Black. A group of reformers proposed to bring to Nashoba slaves, purchased for the purpose, to be educated for life in a free society. The reformers were impractical and the community was badly managed. It was deserted within five years and such few Blacks as were there were transported to Haiti.

If few individual Blacks of this period are well known today, it is not surprising. Many had been transported unwillingly into a completely alien culture. Others, even though born in the United States, had little opportunity to follow the paths that lead to advancement and acknowledgment. Indeed, in some states it was against the law to teach a slave to read and write, although such laws were often disregarded. A few achieved success in the white world, nevertheless.

Paul Cuffe (1759–1817), son of a Black and an Indian, was a free Massachusetts man who became a successful shipowner, operating several vessels and making a modest fortune. He, too, was an advocate of returning Blacks to Africa and in 1815 he made a trip to Sierra Leone, taking with him at his expense nine families. Like others, Cuffe found colonization too expensive to be practical. Frederick Ira Aldridge (1805–1867) was the first Negro actor of importance. A free New York Black, he made his debut in an all-Negro cast while in his teens. Later he was a success all over Europe. Anonymous, as parts of groups, were the Blacks who fought in the War of 1812, in both the army and the navy. At least 10 per cent of Commodore Perry's crews at the Battle of Lake Erie were Black, while two units of Negro troops held strategic positions at the Battle of New Orleans.

For the slaves, as for the Indians, conditions grew worse rather than better between 1800 and 1825. The slave was not in as much danger of being killed or of starving to death after being driven off land, but otherwise the slave, too, was completely at the mercy of white society.

11   Literature and the Theater

THE UNITED STATES in 1800 could lay claim to an intellectual life of its own, even though the foundation came from America's European legacy. Thought, language and literature were formed basically on the British model, but with contributions from other nations—especially the French Enlightenment which had so much effect on men like Jefferson. Dutch and German influences were at work, too, as a result of immigration from those lands.

On the other hand, American intellectual life was shaped and made different from Europe's by the physical environment and the first two centuries of settlement. A completely new world, almost entirely wilderness, and inhabited by a kind of people unknown to Europe, could not help but affect the way men thought about their circumstances and their future. Many Americans, in addition, were culturally patriotic and wanted a distinctive American culture, divorced from the old world. Given the centuries of inherited culture and the tradition of a cosmopolitan intellectual life that cut across national boundaries, this was difficult, but not impossible.

The first quarter of the century, both here and abroad, was a period in which one cultural style was going out and another coming in. The neoclassical style of the eighteenth century, based on the rational, formal elegance of Greek and Roman civilization, was declining. Moving in was romanticism which favored emotion and imagination over logic and rules. America, more than Europe, was the proper setting for romanticism, which idealized the "noble savage" and the unexplored forests and rivers.

American intellectuals who attempted to advance America's cultural independence were sometimes attacked from two directions. The people who went west as pioneers were inclined to express disdain for intellectuals back east who in their eyes were doing nothing useful. The settlers had too many pressing day-to-day problems to be concerned about neoclassicism or romanticism, yet once a town of any consequence grew up, libraries, literary societies, bookshops and other symbols of the life of the mind quickly moved in. From the other side of the Atlantic came harsh attacks by literary critics and by British travelers who had visited the United States. They took a patronizing air and their assaults on American intellectual pretensions were even fiercer after the War of 1812. To the British, America seemed a conceited and braggart nation which had senselessly fought the British right at the time they were locked in a desperate battle with despotism in the form of Napoleon I.

As late as 1820 Sydney Smith, English clergyman and wit, in an article in the *Edinburgh Review,* looked down on everything American:

> During the thirty or forty years of their independence, they have done absolutely nothing for the Sciences, for the Arts, for Literature, or even for the statesman-like studies of Politics or Political Economy. . . . In the four quarters of the globe, who reads an American book? or goes to an American play? or looks at an American picture or statue? What does the World yet owe to American physicians or surgeons? What new substances have their chemists discovered? or what old ones have they analyzed? What new constellations have they discovered by the telescopes of Americans?— what have they done in mathematics? . . . Finally, under which of the tyrannical governments of Europe is every sixth man a Slave, whom his fellow-creatures may buy and sell and torture?

America wasn't as backward in the arts and sciences as Smith described it, either as to institutions or men. The American Philosophical Society, already more than half a century old in 1800, was a truly distinguished organization, contributing to both science and the humanities. Most cities were establishing—or already had established—museums and libraries. A new generation of American scholars was coming of age to join university faculties and to contribute to scholarship. A growing interest in German culture and especially in German universities resulted in a steady stream of young American men going overseas to study. Among them were George Ticknor (1791–1871), Edward Everett (1794–1865) and George Bancroft (1800–91). All three studied at Gottingen, Bancroft receiving his doctor of philosophy degree when he was only twenty. All three returned to teach at Harvard. Ticknor improved the teaching of modern languages. Everett went on to become president of Harvard, governor of Massachusetts, and secretary of state. Bancroft held cabinet and diplomatic positions, and wrote a ten-volume history of the United States.

Most authors and editors of the time wanted a distinctive American literature, free from dependence on British style and tastes. This, however, was difficult, given a common language and much common history. How could American literature be nationalistic when the history of the nation was so short compared with that of Europe? Were American Indians, the frontier, the expanse of nature worthy subjects for serious literature? Some people, even those who wanted to Americanize literature, were not sure. One author, James Kirke Paulding, thought that more was required than "dwelling on scenes and events connected with our pride and our affections." An American author must also indulge in "those little peculiarities of thought, feeling and expression which belong to every nation."

Europe found no American authors worth praising or reading until after the turn of the century. Then, the first and foremost for most of the quarter century was Washington Irving (1783–1859) of New York, the youngest of eleven children of a prosperous merchant. He earned quick recognition with *Letters of Jonathan Old-style, Gent.* (1802–03), which he wrote originally for a newspaper edited by one of his brothers. The series consisted of satires on New York society. A similar series, in which he was joined by some of his friends as coauthors, appeared in 1807–08 as *Salmagundi.* His reputation went up still more in 1809 with the publication of *History of New York,* presumably written by one Diedrich Knickerbocker. It was a sparkling piece of comic literature which, under the guise of a history of New York when it was Dutch, was critical of Jeffersonian democracy from the Federalist point of view. For some years after that Irving dropped literature and, among other things, tried to run the Liverpool, England, branch of his family's business which was headed for bankruptcy. Returning to literature, Irving achieved an international reputation with the publication in 1819–20 of *The Sketch Book,* which contained his versions of legends such as that of Rip Van Winkle and the headless horseman of Sleepy Hollow. Irving's career continued for many years, both as an author and in such posts as minister to Spain. Irving was a well-to-do young man who began writing as a hobby, but his graceful manner and his attention to stylistic perfection made him successful and admitted him to the ranks of authors of international recognition.

Irving was the center of the Knickerbocker group of New York writers who took a sophisticated, satirical, but not unkind, view of society and who were basically conservative and Federalist in their political opinions. Among them was James Kirke Paulding (1778–1860), who collaborated on *Salmagundi.* From the same comic point of view as Irving's *History of New York,* Paulding in 1812 wrote *The Diverting History of John Bull and Brother Jonathan,* about the growth of the colonies. A long poem, *The Backwoodsmen* (1818), was an early example of the prose and poetry written in the nineteenth century with the frontiersman as hero. Unlike most of the group, Paulding was a Jeffersonian and this point of view shows up in such works as *John Bull in America* (1825).

Fitz-Greene Halleck (1790–1867) was another leading member of the Knickerbocker group, as well as personal secretary to John Jacob Astor. The 1819 publication in two New York City newspapers of the "Croaker Papers," which were satirical poems on topics of current interest, brought favorable comment. Halleck's collaborator on the papers was Joseph Rodman Drake (1795–1820), whose only writing published during his lifetime this was, and who died of tuberculosis at an early age.

America's first major novelist, James Fenimore Cooper (1789–1851), came of a well-to-do family, served three years as a midshipman in the United States Navy, then married and settled down as a country gentleman. His writing career began in 1820 with a routine novel called *Precaution,* which followed the style of the conventional English novel of the day. The next year, however, *The Spy* appeared, and the direction of Cooper's career was set. The story of a spy during the American Revolution, the novel was a success almost at once. Then in 1823 came *The Pioneers,* the first of the five famous "Leather-Stocking Tales," which was followed in 1826 by the best known of all, *The Last of the Mohicans.* Cooper used the American frontier experience and the American wilderness for all they were worth. Although his heroes and villains are all good or all bad, and the dialogue is stilted, Cooper was truly an American writer and a marvelous storyteller.

William Cullen Bryant (1794–1878), born in Massachusetts, was a leading literary figure until well past mid-century. As a youth of fourteen he was a strong Federalist and wrote *The Embargo* (1808), an attack on Jefferson's policies. Although not then published, two of his best poems, "Thanatopsis" and "To a Waterfowl," were written before he was twenty-one. Bryant moved to New York in 1825 and was a magazine and newspaper editor there for over fifty years. His move was one of many indications that, by the mid-1820's, New York had succeeded Philadelphia as the literary center of the nation. Bryant was a reformer, a defender of human rights and strongly antislavery. His influence as an editor and critic was felt by all American writers.

A number of men collectively known as the Connecticut (or Hartford) Wits were important in the late eighteenth and early nineteenth centuries, but are almost unread today. Their activities centered around Yale College and Connecticut. Although they tried to modernize the Yale curriculum and were fiercely devoted to making American literature stand on its own feet, they were conservative politically. Perhaps the two most significant members of the Wits were Timothy Dwight (1752–1817) and Joel Barlow (1754–1812).

Dwight, more than anyone else, was the founder of the Wits, his leadership coming from his position as a clergyman and educator, as well as a poet. Of his poetry, *Greenfield Hill* (1794) is an attempt to show that the American scene provided suitable subject matter for poetry. His account of *Travels in New England and New York,* published in four volumes in 1821–22, is an indispensable record of the times as well as a pleasant tale of his journeys. An outspoken defender of orthodox Congregationalism, Dwight was sometimes called the "Protestant Pope of New England." He preached on many subjects, including a sermon on the "Folly, Guilt and Mischiefs of Dueling" in 1805 after the duel in which Burr, who was Dwight's cousin, killed Hamilton. Dwight was president of Yale for twenty-two years.

Barlow, besides being a teacher and a writer, became a diplomat and spent a number of years abroad, during which time he changed from a conservative to a democrat in politics. What he considered his major work was the epic poem, *The Columbiad,* published in 1807, a revision of an earlier work. It attempts to show the glorious future of the United States and its position as the hope of mankind. The poem runs to 8,350 lines and as one critic has said, it is "tedious and turgid." While minister to France, Barlow was invited to join Napoleon I, who was then deep in Russia, to negotiate a commercial treaty. He did so in the fall of 1812, in the midst of Napoleon's disastrous retreat from Moscow. Barlow caught pneumonia from exposure to the bitter weather and died near Cracow, Poland, on Christmas Eve.

An assortment of American authors, some of them almost unknown today, played roles in their day, had their readers and in one way or another contributed to the national literature. Hugh Henry Brackenridge (1748–1816) is an interesting example. Born in Scotland, he was brought to this country, became a clergyman, then gave that up in 1781 to become one of the first settlers of Pittsburgh and a lawyer and judge there. A prolific writer, he began a novel *Modern Chivalry* in 1792, when two parts of it were published. Two more parts followed, then all four were revised in 1805 and an additional volume issued in 1815. While *Modern Chivalry* is hardly readable by today's standards, it does have the distinction of being the first long work of fiction to depict life in the American backwoods. Brackenridge was an enthusiastic supporter of Pittsburgh, and predicted it would become the greatest manufacturing center in the nation, if not the world.

Mercy Otis Warren (1728–1814) of Massachusetts, wife of one patriot leader and sister of another, wrote the first substantial account of the Revolution, *History of the Rise, Progress and Termination of the American Revolution,* published in three volumes in 1805 when she was seventy-seven. Mrs. Warren had a lively style and was strongly patriotic, as well as vigorously anti-Federalist. John Adams was her friend, but he didn't like her book because of its Jeffersonian viewpoint. With an air of male superiority, he remarked that history was "not the Province of the Ladies." Mrs. Otis was a pioneer feminist, urging educational opportunities for women and arguing for recognition of the mental equality of the sexes.

Tabitha Tenney (1762–1837) wrote her only novel, *Female Quixotism,* in 1801. It was a satire on the absurd stories then being turned out as "feminine fiction." Mrs. Tenney's heroine tries to be like the heroines of such fiction, who always get married, but she ends up unable to catch a husband.

Charles Jared Ingersoll (1782–1862) was a strong defender of American culture and often compared his country favorably with Europe in this respect. His *Inchiquin* (1810) was published anonymously, and was supposed to be by a Jesuit traveler in America who had favorable things to say of the nation in contrast to most English travelers. The book, predictably, was attacked by British reviewers.

Although unread today except by a few specialists, John Taylor (1753–1824), born in Virginia and known as "John Taylor of Caroline," was the foremost theorist in support of Jeffersonian and agrarian democracy, as well as states' rights. A plain but dignified man, Taylor was the intellectual spokesman for an agricultural America.

William Wirt (1772–1834), a Virginia lawyer, was the author of two books that attracted favorable attention. The first was *Letters of the British Spy* (1803), which was supposedly the friendly observations of a British visitor to the United States, written to a member of Parliament. The second was a biography of Patrick Henry, the Revolutionary patriot, published in 1817, in which Wirt reconstructed Henry's speeches from notes, tradition and his imagination. Wirt was one of the prosecuting lawyers for the United States at the trial of Aaron Burr for treason in 1807, and in 1817 he became attorney general.

James Gates Percival (1795–1856), born in Connecticut, was a doctor, a journalist, a teacher, a geologist and a linguist. He wanted most of all to be hailed as a poet in the vein of romanticism, and he did for a while achieve popularity with his *Poems* (1821). Percival spent part of his life by choice in the New Haven State Hospital for mental patients. Quite a different kind of person was Clement Clarke Moore (1779–1863) of New York City. Moore was a biblical scholar who taught at the General Theological Seminary, which was erected in the Chelsea section of Manhattan on land that had been part of his family's farm, which he gave to the seminary. He is remembered, though, for his charming poem, "Visit from St. Nicholas," which was first printed in 1821. Catharine Maria Sedgwick (1789–1867) wrote conventional, uplifting fiction, but her work did realistically depict the social customs of the early nineteenth century. *A New-England Tale* (1822) is an example. She was an active feminist, although not a radical.

Magazines and their editors had a distinct influence both in literary and political matters, but whatever their viewpoints on domestic affairs, they were almost unanimous in defending American culture from foreign attacks. Many magazines were founded but few survived long. There were about forty in 1810 and nearly a hundred fifteen years later, but they were mostly small and local in circulation. The *Port Folio,* founded in 1801, reached a circulation of 2,000 in its best days. This journal, edited by Joseph Dennie (1768–1812), was violently opposed to Jefferson and what he stood for. Dennie's attacks so infuriated the Jeffersonians that he was arrested and tried on charges of criminal libel in 1805 but was acquitted. The *North American Review,* which was founded in 1815 and existed for 125 years, was concerned more with intellectual affairs than with politics. It was praised even in Great Britain, but its circulation in 1820 was only 600 and its peak was 3,000 in 1826. The first editor was William Tudor (1779–1830), a Boston merchant who satirized over-scholarly writers in "A Dissertation upon Things in General." Edward Everett was another editor of the *North American Review,* as was Jared

Sparks (1789–1866) who later became, at Harvard, the first professor of history in any American university.

Book publishing began in the colonies before the middle of the seventeenth century, but it was well into the eighteenth before many of the items issued were by American authors. In the period from 1800 to 1830, about 50,000 books, pamphlets and magazines were published in the United States. The market, however, remained small by present standards. Most books sold no more than 1,000 copies. The sale and use of books was steadily increasing, however, as shown by the fact that in 1800 there were probably about fifty libraries in the country with a total of 80,000 books, while a quarter-century later, the four largest cities alone contained fifty libraries with perhaps 1,500,000 books. The day of the free public library had not yet arrived. Most of these libraries required payment of some kind, or membership in some organization.

At the start of the century the leading American publisher was Isaiah Thomas (1749–1831), who fought at the Battle of Lexington and Concord in 1775. Matthew Carey (1760–1839), who was born in Ireland and emigrated to Philadelphia in 1784, operated a growing publishing business. Carey was a self-taught economist who devoted most of his later years to writing in support of protective tariffs and the American System. Another new firm that grew into a large publishing house in New York was that of James Harper and his brothers, established in 1817.

Bookseller, author, preacher, Mason Locke (Parson) Weems (1759–1825) was one of Carey's most active agents as well as a best-selling biographer. He was a traveling peddler of books for thirty years and found time to write several biographies, the only one remembered today being *The Life and Memorable Actions of George Washington*. In the fifth edition, in 1806, Weems first told the story of young George chopping down his father's cherry tree. This, like many incidents in Weems's biographies, came fresh from the imagination of the author. His life of Washington sold steadily for years, probably reaching a total of 50,000 in its first ten years. Weems also wrote uplifting tracts, such as *The Drunkard's Looking Glass* (1812).

Since Weems had sold the copyright in his biography of Washington to Carey, he didn't make much money out of it. Authors found writing a hard way to make a living, and most of them were also clergymen, lawyers, office holders or had some other source of income. Bryant as a young author was satisfied with $2 for a poem. Publishers found it more profitable to push the works of British writers. The absence of an international copyright agreement meant that Americans could publish Sir Walter Scott's novels, for example, without paying him anything. This, however, accounted only in part for Scott's popularity in the United States, which was far greater than that of any other author, American or otherwise. About half a million copies of his novels were sold in the states by 1823. Matthew Carey hired fast boats to go out to meet ships coming from England with a new Scott novel. Thus he could get it printed and on the market ahead of rivals, even if only by a few hours.

Theater-going rose in popularity after the Revolution, as cities grew larger and so were better able to support such activities. At the same time, the prejudice against the theater as immoral was dying out, aided late in the eighteenth century by the lively interest taken by President Washington. Shortly before 1800, new theaters were built in Boston, New York, Philadelphia and Charleston. Permanent acting companies were established and a few cities were large enough to support more than one troupe. The new western cities were able shortly to see theatrical performances, while the national capital had its first theater in 1800. In Pittsburgh there was a theater seating 400 people in 1812; St. Louis was entertained by a company of actors in 1820; and a touring theatrical company made Lexington, Kentucky, one of its stops as early as 1810.

The newer playhouses were large, holding many more people

than twentieth-century theaters designed for the legitimate stage. The Park Theatre, second of the name, that opened in New York in 1821, had a pit, three tiers of boxes and a top balcony and could accommodate 2,500 persons. The Bowery Theatre, built a few years later, was lighted by gas and held 3,500. Around 1800 one New York theater charged from $1 to $2 for admission, the boxes costing the most. Audiences were frequently noisy and rowdy, and on occasion rioted if they didn't like a performance. The pit was the worst spot, with backless benches and a lack of decorum such that women were usually not allowed there. The pit in one theater "was pervaded by evil smells." The top gallery was little better and here Blacks were railed off in a separate section. The boxes, presumably the choice area, were not much more satisfactory so far as comfort went, the seats being so crowded together that a spectator could hardly move.

Most of the leading actors seen on the American stage were from the British theater. One of the first to come to the United States was Joseph Jefferson (1774–1832), who arrived in 1795 and spent the rest of his career in Boston, New York and Philadelphia. Jefferson was the founder of a notable acting family. George Frederick Cooke (1756–1812) had a successful career before coming to America only two years before he died. He was at first very popular, but his heavy drinking made him undependable and his audiences deserted him. Cooke excelled at playing villains, such as Richard III and Iago. Edmund Kean (1787?–1833), one of the most popular actors on both sides of the Atlantic, marked the shift from the restrained, formal acting of the classical school to the more violent and emotional stage portrayals of the romantic style. Kean first visited the United States in 1820–21 and was well received until he broke an engagement in Boston. He regained most of his popularity on a return visit in 1825. Kean played many parts in Shakespearean dramas.

Junius Brutus Booth (1796–1852) rivaled Kean in such roles as Richard III. He was an imposing and rugged figure who brought strength to tragic roles. Booth made his first American appearance in Richmond, Virginia, in 1821 and spent most of the rest of his life in the United States. He had three sons, who all went into the theater and one, John Wilkes Booth, assassinated President Abraham Lincoln. Edwin Forrest (1806–72) was the first notable native-born actor. Born in Philadelphia, he made his professional debut there at the age of fourteen. His acting was forceful, although he was accused of ranting at times, but he gave excellent performances as Lear, Hamlet and Macbeth.

Playwrights and managers were necessary, as well as theater buildings and actors. Those who wrote for the stage and those who ran the theaters spearheaded the movement to have plays express the new nationalistic feeling and to use American themes. This development paralleled the trend in literature. William Dunlap (1766–1839), born in New Jersey, began his career as a portrait painter (he painted both George and Martha Washington), but found the theater more exciting and turned to writing for the stage. His tragedy, *André* (1798), based on an incident in the Revolution, was the first American play to use native material. Dunlap was also a theater manager several times, usually without financial success. He shifted back and forth between the theater and painting, but was the first American to make a serious business of writing for the stage.

James Nelson Barker (1784–1858) was born in Philadelphia and wrote ten plays, several of which were quite good. *The Indian Princess* (1808) was the first play to use the story of the Indian maiden, Pocahontas, who according to tradition saved the life of Captain John Smith. This play was also the first by an American to be performed in England, in 1820. *Superstition* (1824), a tragedy set in New England, is considered Barker's best play and showed his continuing interest in using American themes.

Mordecai Manuel Noah (1785–1851), born in Philadelphia, was a journalist, a politician and a government official as well as a playwright. He, too, used American subject matter in his plays, the first of which was produced in 1812. In 1820, while *The Siege of Tripoli* was playing at the Park Theatre in New York, the theater burned down. *The Grecian Captive* (1822) featured a spectacular stage entrance by the hero and heroine, riding an elephant and a camel respectively. As special agent for the government in Algiers, 1813–15, Noah secured the release of Americans being held prisoner by the Algerian pirates. He had a plan at one time to buy Grand Island, just above the falls in the Niagara River, and turn it into a refuge for Jews from all over the world.

John Howard Payne (1791–1852), born in New York City, was both an actor and a playwright. He wrote the first of his sixty or so plays when he was fifteen and he began his acting career three years later. He was admired as Hamlet and Romeo. In the latter role he played opposite Edgar Allan Poe's mother as Juliet in 1809, the year the author was born. Payne moved to England in 1813 where his popular song, "Home, Sweet Home," was first heard in 1823 in an opera for which he wrote the libretto, *Clari, or the Maid of Milan.* The music was an arrangement of a Sicilian air.

The first acting group of Blacks, the African Company, began giving performances in New York City in 1821. Both Shakespearean drama and lighter plays were produced. Songs in what was supposed to be Negro dialect were heard as early as 1802 in a play called *A New Way to Win Hearts*. Edwin Forrest appeared in blackface in a play in 1823 and the critics praised his performance as the first realistic interpretation of a Negro from a southern plantation. No white actress at the time would blacken her face to play opposite Forrest, so he engaged a Negro washerwoman for the part.

Although not many of the novels, poems or plays of the early nineteenth century are read today, a survey of the period indicates much earnest effort and enthusiasm for putting into books or on the stage, facts and feelings about the young nation. The use of American themes and the justification of American arts and letters as standing on their own feet, apart from Europe, sometimes took precedence over the manner and style of the writing. The best results were seen in the work of Irving, Cooper and Bryant, but in their day there were others who deserved credit also.

12 Music, Art and Architecture

In music, in art and in architecture, as in literature and the theater, the opposing influences of the European legacy and the new national spirit were present in the first part of the nineteenth century. Music reflected Continental influence more than British, and showed less Americanization than did art or architecture. Artistic and architectural styles were heavily influenced by Great Britain. The decline of neoclassicism and the rise of romanticism were apparent, although the latter was late in reaching architecture. American themes, especially the American landscape, received more attention in art as time went on, while the needs of a frontier society and the materials available played a part in the way architecture developed.

The music heard in the United States was mostly foreign, both as to composers and performers, when professionals were concerned. Choral societies were popular, stimulated by the increase in congregational singing in church services. Serious interest in music was indicated by the organizing of the Handel and Haydn Society of Boston in 1815. This society asked the composer Ludwig van Beethoven to compose something for it. Portland, Maine, had a Beethoven Society in 1819, while in 1820 the Musical Fund Society was formed in Philadelphia to help needy musicians as well as to give concerts.

Musical interest spread westward as fast as the frontier. In Lexington the Kentucky Musical Society gave a concert of both instrumental and vocal music as early as 1805, and the Apollonian Society was well regarded in Pittsburgh in 1807. Anthony Philip Heinrich (1781–1861), who was born in Bohemia, came to America in 1816. When his family lost its money, Heinrich went by foot from Philadelphia to Pittsburgh and on into Kentucky. There, beginning in 1817, he gave concerts in which he was at times composer, conductor, violinist and pianist. On one of these occasions a Beethoven symphony was played for the first time in the United States. New Orleans was the only city with a regular season of opera, while Italian opera was introduced to New York audiences in 1825 with a performance of *The Barber of Seville*.

The music the Blacks brought with them from West Africa was heard mostly in their own quarters and in the cotton fields. Negro work chants were not unlike the style of hymn singing in the evangelical churches. West African music was combined with elements from such singing in the Negro spiritual, which was in the process of development. The more popular hymns, which people sang with gusto to tunes they knew well, were written down and published. Jeremiah Ingalls (1764–1828) brought out such a collection in 1805 as *The Christian Harmony*. The first American piano was manufactured in 1775, but even in 1800 no more than fifty pianos, foreign or domestic, could be found in the whole city of Boston. Jonas Chickering of Boston in 1823 began producing pianos on a commercial scale. He devised a cast-iron frame that made it possible for his instruments to withstand the perils of rough journeys to the frontier.

The two individuals who most influenced music in America worked mainly in Boston. Gottlieb Graupner (1767–1836) was born in Germany and emigrated first to Great Britain, and then to the United States in 1795. After playing in an orchestra in Charleston, South Carolina, he moved to Boston in 1798 where for a quarter of a century he was a leading figure in the musical world. About 1801 he organized the Philharmonic Society, consisting of sixteen musicians, both professionals and amateurs. The society gave concerts until 1824. To celebrate the signing of the Treaty of Ghent ending the War of 1812, all Boston's choral and orchestral groups combined in 1815 to give a Peace Jubilee concert. This event in turn led to the organizing of the Handel and Haydn Society, of which Graupner was a founder.

Lowell Mason (1792–1872) was born in Massachusetts and became seriously interested in music while working in a Savannah, Georgia, bank. At that time he compiled *The Boston Handel and Haydn Society Collection of Church Music,* published in 1822. Mason moved to Boston in 1827 to direct the music of three churches, and spent a good deal of his career from then on introducing music education into the Boston public schools. Mason composed the music for many hymns, including "From Greenland's Icy Mountains" and "Nearer My God to Thee."

Compared with the number of people in other skilled and intellectual professions, an unusually large number of artists appear to have been active in the early nineteenth century. Without photography, and with no quick way to make high-quality reproductions of pictures, artists were in demand, and a fair number made a good living. Portraits were wanted to preserve likenesses, while historical events could be recorded only by an artist with pencil or brush. All over America, as the natural wonders of the continent unfolded, more artists turned to depicting the charms and wonders of the landscape. American artists studied abroad, and so style and technique came from Great Britain and the Continent. At the same time, as in literature, the preferred style was shifting from neoclassicism to romanticism.

Among the older generation of painters in 1800, the leading figures were Benjamin West (1738–1820), Charles Willson Peale (1741–1827), Gilbert Stuart (1755–1828) and John Trumbull (1756–1843). West was said to have been introduced as a boy to the use of

colors by an Indian chief in Pennsylvania. In any event, he set up
as a portrait painter when he was eighteen. Four years later he went
to Europe, studied on the Continent and then settled in England in
1763, never to return to his native land. He was such a success that
he became official historical painter to King George III, and succeeded Sir Joshua Reynolds as president of the Royal Academy. West
painted elaborate canvases in the neoclassical style, but by 1800 his
work showed strong romantic tendencies, as in "Death on a Pale
Horse" (1802). His "Franklin Drawing Electricity from the Sky,"
painted about 1805, foreshadowed the romantic style applied to portrait painting. West was always generous with advice and assistance
for young American painters who went to Great Britain to study.

Peale was an amazingly versatile man who was not only a painter
but also a naturalist, an inventor and a museum-keeper. He studied
under West in England for two years, his only formal training. His
1772 portrait of Washington is the earliest-known portrayal of the
first president. Peale was an officer in the Revolution and then settled down to a successful career as a portrait painter. In 1784 he
established Peale's Museum in Philadelphia, which was moved in
1802 to Independence Hall. Besides portraits of revolutionary war
heroes, Peale's museum contained Indian relics, stuffed birds and
animals, including a wild turkey, and odds and ends from the Far
East, among them the kind of birds' nests used in making soup. For
all that, Peale's collection was not a hodgepodge of purely entertaining items. It was carefully arranged and imparted a good deal of information to visitors. Peale was a century ahead of anyone else in
arranging stuffed birds and animals in lifelike positions in a natural-
looking environment.

One of the features of the museum was the reconstructed skele-
ton of a mastodon, a prehistoric mammal. In 1801, when Peale heard
of the discovery of the bones of a very large creature on a farm in
New York State, he organized the first scientific expedition in Ameri-

can history. He carefully supervised the digging-up of the bones, took them to Philadelphia and put them together to make the most awe-inspiring of all his exhibits. Five years later he painted a scene showing the work of excavating the bones. Peale was also busy inventing a velocipede, a new style of eyeglasses, improved false teeth and a polygraph. This last instrument, designed to make it possible to write with two or more pens at the same time, was tried out by Jefferson, with whom Peale was in regular communication on scientific matters. Jefferson promptly sent back drawings showing some suggested improvements.

Peale was the father of seventeen children, of whom four became painters. He named his children after famous painters and scientists: Titian, Rubens, Raphaelle and Rembrandt, for example. Rembrandt Peale (1778–1860) was the best painter among them and became president of the National Academy of Design in 1825.

The most successful American portrait painter was Gilbert Stuart, remembered especially for his portraits of Washington, of which he did 124. Stuart studied in West's studio in London, returning to the United States in 1792 and moving permanently to Boston in 1805. Stuart was very much the pure classical-style painter until 1820, but after that some tendency toward romanticism can be seen. Stuart painted more than 1,000 portraits, including those of the first five presidents of the United States.

Trumbull studied in England and was an American official there from 1793 to 1803. In London again from 1808 to 1816, he was unsuccessful as a portrait painter. Back in the United States he turned to depictions of historical events and received from Congress a commission to decorate the rotunda of the Capitol. Here he did his very large historical paintings, such as "The Signing of the Declaration of Independence" (1818), receiving $32,000 for the four of them.

Among a somewhat younger group of artists were John Vanderlyn (1775–1852), Washington Allston (1779–1843), Thomas Sully

(1783–1872), Samuel F. B. Morse (1791–1872) and Chester Harding (1792–1866). Vanderlyn, the first important American artist to study in Paris rather than London or Rome, was befriended by Aaron Burr who financed five years of study from 1796 to 1801. Later, when Burr fled to Europe after his trial for treason, Vanderlyn was able to assist him. Vanderlyn was a success in France, creating a stir with a nude, "Ariadne," when it was exhibited in 1814. On returning to the United States in 1815, his career collapsed and he became embittered. No one was interested in his large historical paintings and he worked so slowly on his portraits that his sitters lost patience.

Allston, born in South Carolina, studied under West in London and had a satisfactory career there from 1810 to 1818. After his return to America, however, his career declined. He put most of his time and effort into an enormous and never-completed rendition of "Belshazzar's Feast." Allston was important as a leader in the first generation of romanticism. His style was grandiose and dramatic in "The Rising of a Thunderstorm at Sea" (1804). Later, his style became quieter and expressed a mood, as in "The Moonlight Landscape" (1819).

Sully was born in England and came to America with his parents, who were actors. He settled in Philadelphia in 1810 and became the leading portrait painter there. Sully helped create a romantic style of portraiture, giving an effect of grace and sweetness. He is best known, though, for the large historical painting, "Washington's Passage of the Delaware" (1819). A very rapid worker, Sully turned out 2,000 portraits, plus about 500 subject and historical paintings, and some miniatures.

Morse, born in Massachusetts, studied in England under Allston and after his return to the United States in 1815 became well known as a portrait painter. He also liked to paint historical scenes, such as "The Old House of Representatives" (1822). Morse grew more and more interested in electricity rather than painting, and in the early

1830's he turned his attention to devising the telegraph, in which he eventually succeeded.

Harding was a fashionable portrait painter in both London and Boston, but he also traveled west to do portraits of people on the frontier. In Paris, Kentucky, for example, he set up shop and announced he would do portraits for $25 a head. He secured commissions for nearly a hundred as people rushed to the only kind of man who could retain for posterity their likenesses and those of their families. Harding painted aged Daniel Boone in 1819 when he was nearly eighty-five years old, leaning on his long rifle with his dog at his feet.

The style of romanticism, the spirit of American nationalism and the idea of the New World as a second Garden of Eden came together in the manner and subject matter of the Hudson River school of painting. As a group of painters with enough in common to be called a school, this movement started about 1825 and continued for half a century. The Hudson River school was the first American school of landscape painting. It emphasized the grandeur of the landscape, not just picturesque woodland scenes. Three founders and leaders were Thomas Doughty (1793–1856), Asher B. Durand (1796–1886) and Thomas Cole (1801–48).

Doughty, born in Philadelphia, was a self-taught painter, the first American to make a satisfactory career of landscape painting and to be recognized abroad for this. He can be called the first member of the Hudson River school and "On the Hudson" is typical of his work. Durand was born in New Jersey and made a reputation with his engraving of Trumbull's painting of the signing of the Declaration of Independence. He later turned to landscape painting. Cole was born in England and came to America in 1818. On a trip to Ohio he fell in love with the scenery of the country and, returning east, went on a sketching trip in the Hudson River Valley in 1825. The three paintings resulting from the trip established his reputation and did a great deal to popularize the Hudson River school.

John James Audubon (1785–1851) was a combination of naturalist and painter whose work continues to delight nature lovers. Audubon was born in Haiti, studied painting in France and after a few years in the eastern United States, spent nearly twenty years on the frontier. He was determined to find and paint every American bird and, wherever he was, his main effort went toward that purpose. He lived a good deal of the time in Kentucky, keeping a country store which he often neglected to roam the woods looking for more species of birds to paint. He went to England in 1826, hoping to find a publisher who would issue his collection of lifelike paintings of birds. He succeeded, and between 1827 and 1838 four large volumes were published, containing 435 plates reproduced from his art. While Audubon's work was not perfect from the naturalist's point of view, it was a rare combination of art and science.

Miniature painting was popular in the early nineteenth century and continued so until photography took over as a more accurate method of portraying a person. These paintings on ivory, small and delicate, had a charm photographs could never match. Traveling artists, second-rate though some of them were, found business good on the frontier as well as in the cities. Edward Malbone (1777–1807) turned from painting portraits on canvas to the miniature, and his work is notable for its grace. Charles Willson Peale's eldest son Raphaelle and his brother, James, also produced miniatures of distinction.

Sculptors were not very plentiful and the two outstanding American sculptors were largely self-taught. William Rush (1756–1833), born in Philadelphia, was apprenticed as a woodcarver and some of his best work was done in that medium. His 1812 statue, "Spirit of the Schuylkill," was almost destroyed by the elements before it was cast in bronze. His work has a naive but pleasant air about it. John Frazee (1790–1852), born in New Jersey, progressed from cutting tombstones to sculpting portrait busts. He did busts of a number of notable Americans and the one of John Wells (1824) is said to be the first marble bust executed in the United States by a native American.

Several styles and trends were present in the architecture of the early nineteenth century. Among the most handsome buildings existing in 1800, especially in the middle and northern states, were examples of the Georgian style. This style, named for the several Georges who were kings of Great Britain, derived basically from the classical period of Greek and Rome, as interpreted, first, by the Italian Renaissance, and then as modified by English theory and practice in the eighteenth century. Georgian was a formal style, elegant in a regular way, but unpretentious. Red brick was the most commonly used material, at least in the cities. Pilasters or columns at doorways and cornices at the tops of buildings gave a classical touch. After the Revolution, the Georgian style became known as federal in the United States, and some changes took place. Large porticoes became popular features, as did oval, circular and octagonal rooms. The federal style achieved an especially handsome effect when used in the building of large houses, but it was also applied to commercial and government structures.

A new style was becoming popular at this same time and it remained dominant for many years. This was the classic revival, usually called the Greek revival in America. Starting out to imitate the grandeur of Roman architecture, the movement in the United States came to favor the more refined Greek manner. The Greek revival style was thought of as a national style and as a way of showing cultural independence. If the United States was to be a new version of the rational, democratic Greece of ancient times, to copy its architecture was appropriate. This enthusiasm for classical civilization was also displayed in the names of many towns and cities. New York State alone has Rome, Utica, Athens and Troy, to list only four. The Greek revival style was particularly popular in the South, but it spread all over the country, even to the new western towns and cities. It was used for courthouses and farmhouses alike, and for almost every state capitol. It was a relatively simple form of construction and could be done in wood as well as stone. The enthusiasm for Greek architecture, tied as it was to the nationalistic spirit of the times, kept the romantic movement from affecting architecture as early as it did literature. About 1820 there were indications of a change. Buildings, especially churches, began to copy the medieval manner, heralding the arrival of the Gothic revival.

In most parts of the country, wood was used for all kinds of construction because it was easily available and was cheaper than stone or iron. The first textile mills were built entirely of wood, and were as high as five stories in the early 1800's. After 1810, stone was usually used for the outside walls. Home construction varied from the log cabin of the frontier, to the federal and Greek revival mansions of the well-to-do merchants and the southern plantation owners. The log cabin, which was introduced to America in 1638 by Swedish settlers in Delaware, was built throughout the West as the front line of settlement moved along. It could be put up with one tool, an ax, and it required no nails. In spite of the myth that national leaders were all born in log cabins, these rude, uncomfortable structures were not intended as permanent homes and every settler with ambition built something better at the earliest possible moment. Back East, the Cape Cod cottage, with its one and a half stories and gabled roof, was a popular style for those of more modest means than the residents of mansions.

Because of his influence, Thomas Jefferson could well be named America's most important architect of the late eighteenth and early nineteenth century. His own home, Monticello, which he designed, was one of the earliest and best examples of the classical style. Because of his interest, architectural ability and high positions in public office, Jefferson had a great deal to say about the style of a number of public buildings, both in Washington and Virginia. For the state capitol in Richmond, Jefferson sent back designs from France in 1785, based on a Roman temple. His last design, which he worked on between 1817 and 1826, was for the University of Virginia. The focal point of the campus, the library, is almost an exact replica, reduced, of the Pantheon in Rome.

The leading architects of the period were Charles Bulfinch (1763–1844), Benjamin Henry Latrobe (1764–1820), Robert Mills (1781–1855), William Strickland (1788–1854) and Samuel McIntire (1757–1811). Bulfinch's imprint on both public and private buildings in his hometown of Boston set the architectural tone of the city for many years. His use of the classical tradition resulted in simple but elegant buildings, with excellent proportions. Bulfinch worked mostly with brick. He was prolific—designing houses, stores, theaters, hospitals and public buildings. Among these were the Massachusetts State Capitol (1798), University Hall at Harvard (1815) and Massachusetts General Hospital (1820), as well as homes for some of the leading families of Boston. His houses included three different dwellings for Harrison Gray Otis, one of the leaders of the Hartford Convention. From 1818 to 1830, Bulfinch supervised the completion of the Capitol in Washington, which had been in the process of reconstruction since the British burned it in 1814. Enlargement of the structure later caused most of Bulfinch's work to disappear.

Latrobe, who was born in England and who was trained as an architect there and in Germany, practiced his profession before coming to the United States in 1796. He was the first professionally educated architect in the country. His Bank of Pennsylvania building in Philadelphia, completed in 1801, was the earliest Greek revival public building and had wide influence. He designed residences and churches, including the Baltimore Cathedral (1805–1818), the first cathedral in the country. Jefferson appointed him surveyor of public buildings in 1803, and from 1815 to 1817 Latrobe was concerned with the rebuilding of the Capitol. At this time his son Henry went to New Orleans to superintend construction of the city's waterworks which Latrobe had designed. The son died of yellow fever in 1817, and after Latrobe went to New Orleans to take over the work he, too, succumbed to the disease in 1820.

Mills worked with both Latrobe and Jefferson, and was also an enthusiastic exponent of the Greek revival. Mills designed a number of notable monuments, such as the Washington Monument in Baltimore in 1815, in a Greek revival manner, and the Washington Monument in Washington, work on which did not start until 1848. He was a pioneer in trying to build fireproof buildings, the Public Record Office in Charleston (1822–23) being an early attempt. Except for the roof, which was wood sheathed in copper, the building was constructed of stone and brick, with iron used for the window frames, sashes and shutters. The building was unharmed by an earthquake and fire in 1886.

Strickland, born in New Jersey, studied under Latrobe. As a devotee of the Greek revival, he attempted to join the ancient style with the functional needs which his buildings were to fill. When he was thirty he won a competition for the design of the Second Bank of the United States in Philadelphia, and supervised its construction from 1819 to 1824. In this building Strickland used iron for the first time as part of the construction, not just as ornament or in nonstructural parts. Iron rods were introduced as reinforcement in the arched openings at the ends of the vault over the main banking room.

More of a craftsman than a professional architect, McIntire created some of the finest federal-style houses, both as to exteriors and interiors. Born in Salem, Massachusetts, and trained first as a woodcarver, McIntire built luxurious homes for the ship captains and merchant princes of Salem whose ships sailed the seas and captured so much of the trade with the Far East. His masterpiece is the three-story brick house he built for Captain John Gardner in 1804. (It is now known as the Pingree House for a family that later owned it.) A semicircular portico over the front door is supported by slender columns and there is a delicate fanlight over the door. The carved woodwork in the house exhibits McIntire's almost perfect skill in cornices and mantelpieces, with baskets of fruit, sheaves of wheat and horns of plenty.

In music, art and architecture, American theory and practice at the start of the nineteenth century was based largely on British and European models and styles, as might be expected. Yet it is possible to trace the development of distinct American styles and ways of doing things—more so in art and architecture than in music.

13 Education and Religion

OF EDUCATION IN AMERICA in the early nineteenth century, it could be said that there was not enough of it, but that the situation was improving; of religion, that there was plenty, and much enthusiasm for it.

Traditionally, education was the responsibility of the family and the church, but this attitude was changing. The change was prompted by the way the nation thought of itself. In the first place, the United States was a democracy and every citizen needed some education so as to be able to make intelligent decisions at the polls. Secondly, since there was no monarchy or aristocracy to inherit political power, each generation had to educate and develop new leadership to manage the country. People such as Washington and Jefferson put great emphasis on building up a complete educational system.

Of the sixteen states, in 1800 seven had clauses in their constitutions containing general statements about the state's duty to educate the people, and Indiana's new 1816 constitution called for a "general system of education ascending in regular gradations from township schools to a State University, wherein tuition shall be gratis and equally open to all." In actual practice, not too much had been done at the century's start. Opposition to levying local taxes to support free community schools still existed. Every state had some sort of provision for raising money for schools, but most of the laws were inadequate. In the event a parent could not pay the taxes or fees levied, his children were usually permitted to attend school but were labeled "charity" students. The application of this stigma resulted in many poor children not going to school. Nearly half the children in New York City in 1820 were receiving no education because their parents could not pay the required fees. Nevertheless, free elementary education for all, regardless of ability to pay, was on its way, and with it would come secular control of the schools.

At the high-school level no schools entirely supported by public funds existed until the opening of the English Classical School in Boston and the Portland School, in that Maine city, both in 1821. There were other privately supported schools, more or less at the high-school level, and usually called academies. Some received certain public funds, some were in part endowed by the general public or by religious groups. They charged tuition, varied greatly in quality and were slow to admit girls. New York State had thirty-seven academies by 1815, and Massachusetts had thirty.

Teacher-training was nonexistent and the status of teachers low. Few made teaching a career and the quality was often poor. Even an experienced teacher, faced with two score or more students from the age of six up, might have a hard time maintaining discipline. As a result, physical punishment was resorted to regularly. One teacher in Massachusetts in 1810 was paid $8 a month for teaching eighty-six pupils, while in 1820 another received $135 for teaching eighty students for four months.

Considering the era, the population of the country and its newness, the number of colleges in existence in 1800 and the number founded in the next few decades is astonishingly large. Of course, some would not be considered of high academic quality today and they were small, so that there were not many graduates each year. Partly to end dependence on European institutions of higher learning, and partly to ensure the proper kind of education, every administration from Washington's to John Quincy Adams's advocated the establishment of a national university. George Washington left money in his will for such a purpose, and President Madison four times recommended a national university, but a bill drawn up in 1816 failed to get through Congress.

American colleges were established on the British model and most of them were related to one religious denomination or another. There were twenty-two degree-granting institutions in 1800 and the number increased to thirty in 1810, thirty-seven in 1820 and forty-nine in 1830. As late as 1820, though, the novelist James Fenimore Cooper estimated that fewer than 8,000 graduates of the twelve oldest colleges were then living, and that these schools currently enrolled about 3,000 undergraduates. Thus, in spite of the seemingly large number of institutions, the proportion of college-educated men (no graduates were women) in the population was small. One estimate in 1825 was that 1,200 students were studying for the medical profession, 600 for law and 500 for the ministry. The curriculum remained weighted in favor of Greek, Latin, Hebrew, English grammar and logic—although the teaching of science was about to expand rapidly. The founding of colleges in the West went on at a rapid pace, considering the newness of the settlements. Religious enthusiasm and the booster spirit in new states and cities were the cause. The yearly fees for students were high in relation to contemporary prices and incomes: $170 at Harvard and $140 at Yale, for example. Faculty pay in 1800 averaged $600 a year, about the same as for a skilled workman.

Such schools as were available to Blacks were segregated. In the North, some schools were opened by city governments while others were privately established, largely through the efforts of antislavery groups wishing to educate freed slaves and their children. In the South, schools for Blacks were, if not forbidden, at least discouraged, but a few privately sponsored schools functioned. When Boston refused a Negro request for a school in 1800, a group of Blacks started one of their own and hired two Harvard men to teach. The city itself opened an elementary school in 1820. The New York African Free School was established in 1787 and by 1797 there were seven Negro schools in Philadelphia. Several free Blacks combined to build a school in Washington in 1807, but it was 1824 before it had a Black teacher. Such instruction as was available to Negroes was mostly at the elementary level, and for a Black to go on to college was not thought of.

Little education beyond the elementary level was available to women, except for the daughters of the well-to-do who could receive finishing school or private instruction in such social accomplishments as French, music and painting. The careers of three capable and determined women indicated, however, that a change was coming. These women were: Susanna Rowson (1762–1824), Emma Willard (1787–1870) and Catharine Beecher (1800–78). Mrs. Rowson was an actress and author before turning to teaching. Her novel *Charlotte Temple*, published in 1791, was so popular that it went through 150 editions. She opened a school for girls in Boston in 1796 and directed it for twenty-five years. It was one of the best schools of the time.

Mrs. Willard took charge of the Female Academy in Middlebury, Vermont, when she was twenty, and in 1814 opened a school in her home. Here she taught subjects not then offered to women, making it one of the first (perhaps the first) high school for girls. She addressed a stirring and well-argued plea for education for women to the New York State legislature in 1819. In it she remarked tauntingly that history shows many countries

> whose legislatures have sought to improve their various vegetable productions, and their breeds of useful brutes; but none, whose public councils have made it an object of their deliberations, to improve the character of their women.

Governor De Witt Clinton invited Mrs. Willard to move to New York, which she did and founded the Troy Female Seminary, later renamed for her, in 1821. Mrs. Willard was also the author of the popular poem, "Rocked in the Cradle of the Deep," which was later set to music.

Miss Beecher founded the Hartford Female Seminary in 1824 in that Connecticut city and later, in the 1830's, established several schools for girls in the Midwest. She introduced domestic science into her schools and was a strong advocate of liberal education for women. She was, however, opposed to woman suffrage.

Other innovators in education included Thomas Hopkins Gallaudet (1787–1851) who in 1817 founded the first free school for the deaf in the United States at Hartford. He had studied education for the deaf in England and France.

The future of the English language became involved in the debates about the establishment of an American national culture. The purists feared that Americans were departing from the accepted standards inherited from Great Britain. At the other extreme were those who hoped that American-English would depart so far from English-English as to be a separate tongue. Neither extreme had its way, but the American people felt free to experiment with the language, as shown by the coinage of new words and the use of old words for changed meanings.

Noah Webster (1758–1843), author of a spelling book and a dictionary, did more than anyone else to record these changes and to use his influence to Americanize the English language. A veteran of the Revolution and, as a newspaper editor, a Federalist supporter of President Washington, Webster produced a spelling book in the 1780's that was standard in schools for nearly a century and sold several million copies. He compiled a dictionary in 1806, and a much expanded one in 1828. The spelling book and the dictionary made Webster the accepted American authority on spelling and usage. Although he toned down some of his more extreme phonetic changes as time went on, he did introduce such simplified and Americanized spellings as ax, labor and theater. His dictionary was not a record of what the language should be, but a report on it as a living tongue in daily use in the United States.

Religious activity in the early nineteenth century was marked by enormous enthusiasm, expressed through the Great Revival, and by a large amount of shifting, forming and reforming of denominations and sects. The four denominations most involved in the spiritual awakening that swept the country, especially the West, were the Congregationalists, the Presbyterians, the Baptists and the Methodists. The first two were strongest in New England and the middle Atlantic states, while the other two became dominant in the South and West as the revival went on. The Congregationalists and the Presbyterians were bound more by formal creeds than the others and put more emphasis on a well-educated ministry. Among the Baptists and the Methodists, belief in the Bible and personal repentance and salvation were what counted.

Lyman Beecher (1775–1863) filled both Congregational and Presbyterian pulpits and was a perfect example of the kind of clergyman these two denominations favored, although his views were too liberal for some people. He preached a series of six sermons on intemperance that in printed form went through many editions, and in 1816 he helped found the American Bible Society. When tax support was withdrawn from the Congregational Church in Connecticut, Beecher blamed it on "Sabbath-breakers, rum-selling, tippling folks, infidels and ruff-scuff generally." In the early 1830's he went west to be head of a seminary in Cincinnati. Beecher fathered thirteen children of whom six became well known in one way or another. They included Catharine Beecher, mentioned above, and Harriet Beecher Stowe, author of *Uncle Tom's Cabin*.

Adoniram Judson (1788–1850) went to India as a Congregational missionary in 1812, but the next year he became a Baptist and moved on to Burma where he served his faith for thirty years. In the course of his career he translated the Bible into Burmese. Judson had three wives, one who founded a girls' school in Rangoon, one who translated *Pilgrim's Progress* into Burmese, and one who wrote moralistic tracts.

A difficult but effective way of reaching people on the frontier with the message of the Christian religion was devised by the Methodists and was called circuit riding. One minister served a large area of scattered settlements and individual cabins, the number ranging from twenty to forty. He made his rounds on horseback as the only practical way to travel on the frontier, with his belongings and his Bible in his saddlebags. Every four or five weeks he made a complete circuit of his territory, regardless of wild animals, the weather or other hazards. When the weather was stormy, people said: "There is nothing out today but crows and Methodist preachers." The circuit riders preached wherever they found a place and an audience—in homes, in schools and even in barrooms.

The most remarkable circuit riders were Francis Asbury (1745–1816) and Peter Cartwright (1785–1872). Asbury was born in England and was sent to the colonies by the British Methodists in 1771. He became the first American Methodist bishop in 1784, but the heart of his career was his forty-four-year record of preaching. As a circuit rider he traveled about 5,000 miles a year over trails and paths, and his total was at least 250,000 miles. He is said to have converted 300,000 persons and ordained 4,000 Methodist ministers, almost single-handedly making his denomination one of the strongest in the country.

Cartwright was a more colorful character than Bishop Asbury. He was born in Virginia and had no formal education. He was licensed to preach by the Methodists when he was only seventeen. Three years later he was a deacon and, at twenty-two, a presiding elder. Cartwright rode the circuit for nearly fifty years in Kentucky, Tennessee, Indiana, Ohio and Illinois. He had a loud voice and an eloquent tongue, using vivid figures of speech that threatened sinners with hellfire. He ran against Abraham Lincoln for Congress in 1846 and lost.

The Great Revival began in Kentucky about 1797 and spread rapidly, especially in the West where emotional fervor was so great that it resulted in physical manifestations, such as jumping, jerking about and crying out. The Congregationalists and Presbyterians joined forces, but the Baptists and the Methodists were the spearhead of the revival and captured the most converts. The preachers who organized the revival meetings were determined to save the West from its evil ways. Asbury spoke of the "little wicked western trading towns," while evangelists sang:

> Come hungry, come thirsty, come ragged, come bare,
> Come filthy, come lousy, come just as you are.

The heart of the Great Revival was the camp meeting, the first of which was held about 1800. The camp meeting was a large outdoor gathering that lasted up to a week. A platform was erected for the preachers and a few planks across tree stumps provided some seats, but people mostly stood or sat on the ground. Whole families came, bringing their food and bedding and living in tents. Attendance at the large camp meetings ran to several thousand, while a number of preachers were active, taking turns delivering sermons, or several of them preaching simultaneously in different parts of the camp. One meeting in Kentucky had eighteen Presbyterian ministers plus a number of Baptist and Methodist clergymen. In some ways a camp meeting was like a family reunion or a large picnic, and more than one romance got its start there. The serious business, though, was listening to the words of the preachers and singing hymns. The theme was salvation by repenting of one's sins, and being converted so as to sin no more. With the constant theme of threatened damnation, the scary oratory of the ministers worked the audience into a high pitch of emotion, with much shouting, weeping and rolling on the ground. How many camp-meeting converts remained good church members and how many were soon backsliders in need of saving again no one knows, but those who attended these meetings on the frontier during the Great Revival never forgot their experience.

The "inventor" of the camp meeting, if any one person deserves the credit, was James McGready (c. 1758–1817), who also had as much to do as anyone with starting the whole revival movement. A Presbyterian minister from Pennsylvania, McGready's preaching in Logan County, Kentucky, just before the turn of the century, lighted a religious fire that turned into the Great Revival. Someone who heard McGready preach said that he "could so array hell before the wicked that they would tremble and quake, imagining a lake of fire and brimstone yawning to overwhelm them." Another well-known voice at camp meetings was that of Lorenzo Dow (1777–1834) who was at times connected with the Methodist Church, but was usually an independent preacher traveling around on horseback. He became a familiar figure because of his oddities of dress and manner as well as for his pulpit eloquence. Dow introduced the camp-meeting idea into England and Ireland.

Other religious groups, although overshadowed in the Great Revival, were not without place and influence in American religious life. Before the Revolution, the Church of England was powerful among the upper classes in the North and the planter aristocracy of the South. The loyalists who fled the colonies during the Revolution were largely members of the Church, and this, together with the fact that it was the official, established church in England, made the denomination suspect among patriots. Nevertheless, many of the original leaders of the nation, including George Washington, belonged to what became, after independence, the Protestant Episcopal

Church. As one old-fashioned Virginia Federalist remarked: "No *gentleman* would choose any road to heaven but the Episcopal."

In sharp contrast was the Society of Friends, the people commonly called Quakers. Their considerable influence in the United States stemmed from William Penn, the Quaker leader who founded Pennsylvania in the late seventeenth century as a haven. Feeling the need for only an "inward light," the Friends' worship was poles apart from the formal ceremonies of the Episcopalians. A notable member of the Friends was Edward Hicks (1780–1849), a preacher who supported himself by painting signs and carriages. When he felt he was getting too proud of his eloquence as a preacher, he gave it up and turned to painting in a charming, primitive manner. His favorite subject, of which he did about a hundred versions, was "The Peaceable Kingdom," in which animals of all kinds are shown getting along without fighting or eating each other.

The Roman Catholic Church was small and only beginning to grow. In the colonial period, given the strong Protestant background of Great Britain and of the large majority of the settlers, Catholics had not fared well. Only in Maryland and Pennsylvania were they free to worship. The first Catholic Bishop was John Carroll of Baltimore, who was made bishop in 1790. In the whole country in 1807 there was only one diocese, with seventy priests, eighty churches and a membership of 80,000. The Louisiana Purchase added considerably to Catholic strength since New Orleans, with its French background, was largely Catholic. By 1830 there were ten dioceses, six seminaries, nine colleges, thirty-three monasteries and houses of religious women, and many schools.

The Disciples of Christ, or Campbellites, came into existence in this period, formed by a splitting-off of members of the Presbyterian, Baptist and Methodist churches. Thomas Campbell (1763–1854) and his son Alexander (1788–1866) were the co-founders. After differences of opinion about church practices with the Presbyterians, Thomas and his followers withdrew and formed the Christian Association in 1809. Alexander soon joined his father and eventually a new denomination came into existence.

Unitarianism has a historical background stemming from the sixteenth century, but as a denomination in America, it grew out of differences of belief within the Congregational Church (and, to a lesser extent, the Episcopal Church) in the late eighteenth and early nineteenth centuries. By 1815 liberal Congregationalists founded a new denomination and in 1825 the American Unitarian Association was officially formed. Henry Ware (1764–1845) was one of the fathers of Unitarianism. When he was appointed to teach theology at Harvard in 1805, his known liberal views brought strong opposition from conservative Congregationalists and hastened the split. William Ellery Channing (1780–1842), who from the time he was twenty-three until his death was pastor of the Federal Street Church in Boston, became the leading spokesman for the Unitarians. A sermon he delivered in Baltimore in 1819 explaining his views earned him the title of "apostle of Unitarianism."

If they were interested in religious worship and church membership, Blacks had problems, whether they were free Negroes in the North or slaves in the South. In the North, even though slavery was ending, the practice of admitting Negroes to white churches began to end. When some churches introduced segregated seating, the Blacks withdrew and formed their own churches. In Philadelphia, with Bishop Asbury's blessing, Richard Allen (1760–1831) organized the African Methodist Episcopal Church in 1787 after whites in the church where Allen sometimes preached tried to make Negroes sit in the gallery. There were sixteen congregations by 1816 in a formal organization and Allen became the first bishop. Four years later there were 4,000 Negro Methodists in Philadelphia alone. In the same way, in 1809 and also in Philadelphia, Blacks formed a Baptist church. In the South, however, no formal church groups sprang up. In some cases, slaves worshiped in church with the owner and his family, sitting separately of course. On some plantations informal religious services were held by Blacks. Slave owners worried about Blacks assembling in meetings for fear they would use the opportunity to conspire against them. They never permitted any Black preacher to acquire much of an education, although religious services were usually encouraged because they gave the slaves an emotional outlet.

Several small sects and groups added variety to America's religious life, such as the Adventists whose beliefs centered on the second coming of Christ. One Adventist, a young New York farmer named William Miller (1782–1849), in 1818 predicted the end of the world for 1843. The Shakers originated in England, splitting off from the Quakers and following their leader "Mother" Ann Lee to America in the late eighteenth century. New converts were made and by 1826 there were Shaker communities as far west as Indiana. George Rapp (1757–1847), a German religious leader, brought his followers to the United States in 1803 and in 1814, as the Harmony Society, founded the community of Harmony in Indiana. It was an authoritarian, cellbate group that declined after Rapp's death. Another small German separatist group, whose leader was Joseph Michael Bimeler (1778–1853), arrived in 1817 and founded Zoar in Ohio, a communal settlement.

Finally, there was no more zealous patriot or religious advocate than Elias Boudinot (1740–1821), president of the Continental Congress in 1782–83. He was later director of the United States Mint, and a founder and first president of the American Bible Society. A supporter of philanthropic causes, he adopted a Cherokee Indian as his son. Boudinot expected the end of this world and the coming of the Millennium, in which Christ would reign on earth for a thousand years, very soon. In his tract *Star in the West* (1816) he said the Millennium would begin in the American West and he believed the lost tribes of Israel would be found there.

In no other field was there, perhaps, more change, with promise for the future, than in education and religion in America in the first quarter of the century.

14 Science, Medicine and Law

OF SCIENCE IN AMERICA in the early nineteenth century, it could be said that there was a great deal of interest but few major accomplishments; of medicine, that it was advancing in practical matters but remained weak in theory; of law, that brilliant minds were shaping old concepts to America's needs.

People such as Jefferson believed that unlocking the secrets of nature was an important part of the process whereby people and society would move steadily onward and upward. This faith in science and progress stemmed from the scientific achievements of Isaac Newton (such as the formulation of the theory of gravity) in the seventeenth century, and the rational philosophy of the Enlightenment in the eighteenth. In practice, though, the United States contributed little of importance to science in the first quarter of the nineteenth century. Jefferson, with all his other interests and duties, probably possessed America's best scientific mind. He made contributions in several fields, such as botany, ethnology and meteorology.

Among those whose main concern was science, Samuel Latham Mitchill (1764–1831) and Benjamin Silliman (1779–1864) stand out. Mitchill, American born, was trained at Edinburgh as a physician, taught at the College of Physicians and Surgeons in New York, and edited the first American medical journal of consequence. Like Jefferson, he had a variety of interests. He held several elective offices, including that of United States senator from New York. He also did pioneer research in geology, botany and zoology. As the historian Henry Adams wrote of him: "Dr. Mitchill could have filled in succession, without much difficulty, every chair in Columbia College as well as in the Academy of Fine Arts about to be established." In this period a number of scientists such as Mitchill were originally trained as physicians because science was taught mostly in medical schools.

Silliman, a chemist, geologist and physicist, devoted his career more specifically to science. A graduate of Yale, he was appointed when only twenty-three to be the first professor of chemistry and natural history there. His work stimulated other colleges to add science to the curriculum. Silliman was the first to use laboratory instruction in teaching chemistry and in 1818 founded the first important scientific periodical in the country, the *American Journal of Science.*

Joseph Priestley (1733–1804), a co-discoverer of oxygen, although he didn't call it that, emigrated from England in 1794 when feelings against him—because of his sympathy with the French Revolution—became too great for him to stand. He lived the rest of his life in Pennsylvania, continuing his investigations. His arrival stimulated interest in chemical analysis. After trips through the South and in Indian country in the West, William Bartram (1739–1823), a naturalist taught by his naturalist father, wrote his *Travels* (1791). The book was internationally popular and not just for its scientific aspects. Its descriptions of the landscape became a source of inspiration for some of the English romantic poets. Bartram compiled a list of 215 native American birds, the most complete list at the time.

David Hosack (1769–1835) was both a physician and a botanist. As a physician, he taught at the College of Physicians and Surgeons, helped found Bellevue Hospital in New York and was the doctor who attended Hamilton after his duel with Burr. As a botanist he established the Elgin Botanical Garden where Rockefeller Center now stands in midtown Manhattan. Born in Turkey of French and German parents, Constantine Samuel Rafinesque (1783–1840) emigrated to the United States in 1815 and taught both modern languages and botany at Transylvania University in Kentucky. His theories on the evolution of species predated similar work by Charles Darwin, but he was criticized by some fellow scientists for inaccuracy.

Minister of a Congregational church in Massachusetts for thirty years and an orthodox opponent of Unitarianism, Jedidiah Morse (1761–1826) was also "the father of American geography" by virtue of his widely used textbooks in that subject. His geographical knowledge was not exactly complete, as is shown by his statement that "North America has no remarkably high mountains. The most considerable are those known under the general name of the Allegany Mountains." Morse was interested in improving the treatment of the Indians and in 1820 he was appointed by the government to visit several Indian tribes. His report to the secretary of war in 1822 on his trip was a valuable document. Morse wrote a tract entitled *Signs of the Times* in 1810 in which he predicted that the end of the present world and the coming of the Millennium would begin about 1866. Morse was the father of Samuel F. B. Morse.

William Maclure (1763–1840), who was born in Scotland, made a fortune in business in London before visiting the United States several times. After traveling on foot over a large part of the country, he issued his *Observations on the Geology of the United States* in 1809. It and an accompanying map were milestones in the science of geology in America. Amos Eaton (1776–1842) began his professional life as a lawyer, then turned to botany and geology. He carried out a geological survey along the Erie Canal in New York in 1822–23. Earlier, he gave the first course of popular lectures on botany in 1810. In 1824 he began teaching at the technical school established by Stephen Van Rensselaer at Troy, New York.

As an early American ornithologist, John James Audubon is

remembered primarily for the beauty of his drawings of birds. Alexander Wilson (1766–1813), on the other hand, is honored for the scientific value of his ornithological work, although his drawings of the birds he found in the American wilderness are also most attractive. Wilson was born in Scotland and came to America in 1794. He was encouraged in his study of birds by William Bartram and at the same time he taught himself to draw. He did his research by making long, difficult and lonely expeditions on foot. One time he walked in winter weather from Pennsylvania to Niagara Falls. Out of this adventure came not only ornithological knowledge but also a poem 2,200 lines long, *The Foresters* (1804). Another time he hiked to Pittsburgh and then took a boat down the Ohio. To break the monotony of his walking trips he played Scottish airs on his flute as he went along. In all, Wilson discovered thirty-nine species of birds, and on his journeys he met Audubon and gave him advice. The results of his hard work appeared between 1808 and 1814 in the form of nine volumes, *American Ornithology*, the last two volumes of which were finished by a friend after Wilson's death. In reviewing the last five volumes, De Witt Clinton took the occasion to sound a popular American theme:

> The life of Mr. Wilson exhibits the complete triumph of genius over the want of education, and of persevering industry over the evils of poverty. . . . shows, conclusively, that the temple of fame is open to the most humble individual in the community. . . .

Although some practical advances in medical treatment and in surgery were made in the early nineteenth century, medical theory stood still both in the United States and abroad. The germ theory was unknown and so medical scientists could not come up with any general explanation of what caused illness and disease, or how different diseases were related to each other. If one did not know the cause of a disease, it was impossible, except by luck, to find a cure. Bleeding was a favorite practice and draining blood from ill people may have killed nearly as many as disease did. Epidemics of typhoid and yellow fever were frequent and deadly. Some doctors and scientists thought contaminated water and food caused such diseases, and this brought about better public health measures such as street cleaning and sewage disposal. While the actual causes remained unknown, such steps did help. Malaria was associated with swamps, but no one had yet made the connection between mosquitos as carriers and the disease.

Medical education was improving and medical societies and journals helped spread such useful information as became available. Most of the leading doctors in 1800 had had European training, the University of Edinburgh being the medical school with the highest reputation. Six medical schools existed in the United States and more were being founded, especially in the West, so that fewer Americans studied in Europe. Most doctors at the turn of the century, however, gained their education by the apprenticeship system, which meant that their knowledge was limited to the skill and practice of the physician to whom they attached themselves. The first *United States Pharmacopoeia*, giving such information as was known about the qualities and usages of drugs, appeared in 1820, the work of a committee headed by Dr. Mitchill.

Considering the state of medical science, the United States had a respectable number of medical men who met the highest standards of the time and who contributed some practical improvements in medicine and surgery. A distinguished leader of his profession in New York was Samuel Bard (1742–1821), who was educated at Edinburgh. He was a founder of the medical school of King's College (Columbia) in 1767 and was its dean from 1792 to 1807. He also helped organize New York Hospital, wrote a manual on midwifery and a forward-looking report on medical education.

A signer of the Declaration of Independence when he was thirty-one, and a Jeffersonian in politics while remaining a friend of Federalist John Adams, Benjamin Rush (1745–1813), of Pennsylvania, was another of the versatile men of his time. While his profession was medicine, he was the first professor of chemistry in the country, treasurer of the United States Mint in Philadelphia from 1797 until his death, and a founder of the first antislavery society. When a yellow fever epidemic struck Philadelphia in 1793 he remained in the city all through it, caring for the victims. He was such a strong advocate of large-scale bleeding and purging of the ill, however, that some who used bleeding in a more restricted manner disagreed with his methods. Rush was a pioneer in the study of mental disorders, his paper of 1812 being the earliest clinical work on the subject.

Benjamin Waterhouse (1754–1846), a Boston physician and the first professor of medical theory and practice at Harvard University in 1783, introduced from England in 1800 Dr. Edward Jenner's method of vaccination against smallpox. To offset the opposition to it on the part of some people, including certain medical men, Waterhouse solicited Jefferson's assistance. Always interested in scientific advances, Jefferson had Waterhouse send him a supply of vaccine at Monticello. He then proceeded, with the aid of a local doctor, to vaccinate his family, his slaves, anyone else on his plantation and even some of his neighbors. Before he returned to Washington about two hundred people had been vaccinated.

Nathan Smith (1762–1829), who helped found Yale's medical school, wrote a *Practical Essay on Typhus Fever* in 1824, while Caspar Wistar (1761–1818) wrote the first American textbook on anatomy in 1811–14. The first professor of surgery at the University of Pennsylvania, Philip Syng Physick (1768–1837) performed many operations for cataracts and improved the methods of treating fractures. Ephraim McDowell (1771–1830) practiced medicine in Kentucky and in 1809 performed the first ovariotomy (removing an ovary) on record. He was also noted for his success in lithotomy (removing stones from bladders). John Collins Warren (1778–1856), who taught at the

Harvard medical school for forty years and who in 1811 was one of the founders of Massachusetts General Hospital, was the first surgeon to operate on a strangulated hernia. Operations such as these are commonplace today, but in the early nineteenth century they were dangerous and difficult because of the lack of knowledge and the absence of modern equipment and anesthetics.

A unique opportunity to advance knowledge of the human body came to an army surgeon, William Beaumont (1785–1853). While he was serving at an army post on Mackinac Island in the Great Lakes, Beaumont was called on to treat a young man of nineteen whose stomach had been blown open by an accidental gunshot wound at close range. The patient recovered but the wound never entirely healed over. Recognizing his opportunity, Beaumont, beginning in 1825 and for a period of years, studied at first hand the process of digestion. He performed a large number of experiments which threw entirely new light on gastric physiology in the body.

In the legal profession and in the application of the law from the judge's bench, Chief Justice John Marshall was far and away the most influential figure of the period. Yet in the development of legal theory and the adaptation of America's inheritance from British law to the new nation's situation, three other names are of almost equal prominence: James Kent (1763–1847), Edward Livingston (1764–1836) and Joseph Story (1779–1845). Kent was a leading member of the bar in New York State, occupying all the highest judicial positions and teaching at the Columbia College law school. His lectures there were expanded into his *Commentaries on the American Law,* which appeared in four volumes between 1826 and 1830. This work was accepted as the authority on the English common law in the United States, and was consulted and cited everywhere. Kent was a stern Federalist all his life. At the New York constitutional convention in 1821, he vigorously opposed universal suffrage, saying that "it is too mighty an excitement for the moral constitution of men to endure."

Edward Livingston, of the large and powerful Livingston family of New York, began a public career in that state. While he was mayor of New York City, however, a clerk either lost or stole some city funds, and Livingston, feeling responsible, resigned his office and moved to New Orleans. During the War of 1812 he was aide-de-camp to General Jackson, and he also held public office in Louisiana. He was appointed in 1821 to draft a new code of law and of criminal procedure. Louisiana never adopted the code, but it was so complete and so brilliantly executed that Livingston won international fame for it. His code became a model for the penal laws of several states. Livingston's code approached crime from the point of view of remedies rather than punishment.

Joseph Story of Massachusetts was appointed to the Supreme Court of the United States by President Madison when he was only thirty-two years old, the youngest man ever named to the highest bench. He served thirty-four years, until his death. Story and Marshall agreed on a broad interpretation of the Constitution and of the powers of the Federal government. Among other notable opinions was the one Story wrote in 1816, in a case that established the power of the Supreme Court to review issues of constitutional law raised in cases tried in state courts. Story was a strong abolitionist and in several instances ruled that Blacks brought into the country illegally must be repatriated to Africa. Story also taught at Harvard and out of his lectures came textbooks which, with Kent's writings, had the greatest influence on American legal education for many years.

15 Life in America

DOMESTIC POLITICS, foreign affairs, the West, the Indians, slavery—all these were of prime importance in American life during the first quarter of the nineteenth century. But so, too, were matters of more direct concern to the people in the course of their daily lives: social relationships, living habits and standards, reform movements, and changes in the urban environment, to name only some.

American society in 1800 was essentially white, Protestant and British in background. People of other white European nationalities, however, did not need to fear discrimination, and class lines, while they existed, were not very rigid. Political democracy, to which the nation had dedicated itself, implied social democracy as well. There were an upper class, a middle class and a lower class; bosses and workers; masters and servants. But to move from one class to another, especially on the frontier, was not difficult. American servants did not think of themselves as forever fixed in that station in life, as they did in Europe. An ambitious young maid might well expect to have servants of her own some day if she worked hard and married properly.

The status of women was high in theory but not so high in practice. A woman was supposed to be pure, pious, submissive and domestic, and to uphold the standards of the home and of society, which men could not be trusted to do. But although women were supposedly of a higher nature, they had few rights in the society of the time. Once married, a woman was entirely dependent on her husband, who could beat her and the children and who controlled any property his wife brought to the marriage. In practice, though, it often turned out that the wife was the real ruler of the household. Wives were in great demand because of a shortage of women, especially the nearer one got to the frontier.

American children had fewer restraints than European youth. In a busy, growing society, with more work to be done than there were hands to do it, children were expected to take a useful part as soon as they were able. A number of prominent men who have already been mentioned achieved in their late twenties or early thirties high posts or reputations that today go to men in their forties and fifties. Families were usually big, and the number of children born to each marriage was large. The high mortality rate of the time, especially among children, made this necessary if families were to multiply.

The money income of Americans of the early nineteenth century seems exceedingly low by today's standards. However, goods cost far less then, and also many people were not entirely dependent on wages and salaries since they raised some of their own food and made some of their own clothing. A small number of wealthy businessmen had incomes that allowed them to live in luxury. At the other end of the scale, farmers might have no more than $100 a year cash income because they raised most of what they needed. In between, a man of the professional middle class could earn $1,000 a year and live very comfortably on it.

The houses Americans lived in went up the scale all the way from the rude log cabins of the frontier to the federal and Greek revival mansions of the wealthy, but there were as yet few tenements or slums in the cities. Given the universal lack of modern conveniences, such as central heating and electric lighting, the difference between rich and poor homes lay in size and in the quality of the furnishings. Every northern home depended on fireplaces, and the family or its servants had to pump water by hand, or carry it in from the well. Many floors, and not just in cabins, were bare, or painted. In the eighteenth century carpets, quite scarce and expensive, had been used to cover tables. By 1800 they were beginning to be commonly used on floors in upper-class homes. Interior walls were often whitewashed, while wallpaper was popular with those who could afford it.

The preferred style in furniture came from workshops such as that of Duncan Phyfe (c. 1768–1854), who was born in Scotland and set up in business in New York in the early 1790's. He worked mostly in solid mahogany and made chairs, tables, sofas and sideboards, following what was the English style of the time. His earlier work has excellent proportions, graceful curves and simple ornamentation. Later, in the 1820's, he took up the empire style, a name honoring Napoleon I, which was basically classical but had touches of imperial grandeur. Phyfe was merely following the fashion of the times.

French styles by way of Great Britain determined fashion in dress, as they had since colonial days. Under the influence of the romantic movement and the French Revolution, women's fashions became much simpler around the turn of the century. Light dresses, low cut and sleeveless, replaced the elaborate billowing gowns of the old aristocracy. Hair was cut short instead of being piled high in elaborate hairdos. Then, around 1815, fashion began to move back to the era of stiff corsets, leg-of-mutton sleeves and full skirts that developed into the hoop skirt.

Men's fashions changed in the same general way. Knee-length pantaloons, with buckles, silk stockings and low-cut shoes, as well as the wig, were on their way out by 1800. President Monroe was the last chief executive to dress this way, and an 1823 painting of Monroe and his cabinet shows him the only person clothed in the old-fashioned manner. In place of the eighteenth-century style, long trousers came in, reflecting the French Revolution whose supporters from the middle and lower classes dressed this way in contrast to the aristocracy and nobility. The style therefore seemed appropriate for democratic America. Two patents for suspenders to hold up the new pants were granted in 1804. Men wore their hair long for a while yet, tying it back in a queue.

The styles described were those worn by the upper classes or by the professional and middle classes on important social occasions. Workmen and farmers and their families dressed in simpler clothing, much of it made at home and, on the frontier, some of it put together from the hides of animals.

Most Americans had plenty to eat, but few enjoyed a balanced diet. On the farms there was seldom any problem of quantity, and wild game supplemented farm production. Both on the farm and in the city, however, the absence of refrigeration and even of canning until about 1820, meant that much salt pork and other preserved items were staples in the diet. Fresh fruits and vegetables were unavailable a good part of the year. Foreigners were most impressed by the large quantities of greasy food consumed by Americans, and by the speed at which they ate. One visiting French count was nearly made ill by a breakfast which included fish, steak, ham, sausage, salt beef and hot breads. As he saw it: "The whole day passes in heaping indigestions on one another."

Americans enjoyed many forms of recreation. Amusements depended on the section of the country, one's position in life and the attitude of the community toward pleasure. Puritan New England, for example, frowned on such recreations as dancing and such sports as horse racing longer than other parts of the country. The gentlemen of Virginia and their ladies were great devotees of both dancing and horse racing. As late as 1800, travel on the Sabbath was forbidden in Connecticut and Massachusetts, and in Boston in 1806 the old-fashioned minuet was still being danced while the waltz was considered not respectable. Meanwhile, in the South, cock-fighting was popular.

Most Americans had little time for sports or recreation, because of long working hours and, in places, restrictions on what was permitted on Sunday, their one day off. Nevertheless, Americans did find one way or another to enjoy themselves. In the North in winter, ice skating and sleighing were popular both in the country and in the city. In this era, though, as cities grew in size, their inhabitants found it more difficult to participate in such sports as hunting and fishing. At the same time, larger concentrations of people made it possible for professional spectator sports to prosper. On the frontier, recreation and work were often combined in barn raisings where neighbors gathered to help erect a barn. Such affairs were also picnics, often followed by lively barn dances where the activity was far more vigorous than in the ballrooms of upper-class city people.

Marksmanship was highly prized in rural areas and on the frontier, and shooting matches were held with such prizes as a side of beef or a turkey for the best record. Squirrel-shooting competition involved teams of, say, four men each. On one occasion, by nightfall one team had shot 152 squirrels, the other 141. The most brutal sport was the rough and tumble fight, English in origin, and popular in the South and West long after it was rejected by the East. In a rough-and-tumble fight there were no rules and the two contestants were free to bite off ears or gouge out eyes until one or the other gave up, or became unconscious.

Among spectator sports, horse racing was the most popular. Long established in the South, it moved into the North, except for New England. In 1823, two years after New York repealed its ban on horse racing, a match race attracted a crowd estimated all the way from 50,000 to 100,000 to the Union Course on Long Island. Here the northern champion, Eclipse, raced the southern hope, Sir Henry, in two out of three four-mile heats. Eclipse won, taking a purse of

$20,000, and the crowd went wild. Professional footraces were also extremely popular—so much so that they were moved to race courses so that admission could be charged. Henry Stannard became a popular champion when he ran ten miles in just under an hour and won a prize of $1,000. Prizefighting was frowned on, but professional matches were held, usually in as much secrecy as possible. Tom Molyneux, a former Black slave from Virginia, claimed the heavyweight championship of the country, but found it more profitable to do most of his bare-knuckle fighting in England. He lost a match to Tom Cribb in London in 1810.

People seeking amusement in the cities could visit wax museums or public gardens. In the Vauxhall Gardens, located "two miles out on the Bowery Road," New Yorkers in 1807 could hear band concerts and choral singing and watch fireworks. Niblo's Columbian Gardens, also in New York, featured trees and flowers from foreign lands, with sparkling fountains. Other cities had similar amusement parks. The circus, growing out of the English equestrian show, was beginning to take on its later character as mounted clowns, tumblers and high-wire artists were added. After 1815 as many as thirty traveling circuses were on the road in the North and the upper South. They were small, usually boasting no more than six or eight performers. Wild animals from Asia and Africa were exhibited around 1800 in a few places in cities, but had not yet joined the circus. The first elephant was probably brought to the United States in 1796, and it was not long before the great beast with the trunk was the biggest drawing card of traveling exhibits.

Around the turn of the century, the report of the medicinal value of the waters at Saratoga Springs, in New York State, resulted in the growth of a luxurious summer resort for the well-to-do who came from the South as well as the North to enjoy both waters and the social life. A hotel was built at Saratoga as early as 1802, and by 1809 the resort was geared for elegant leisure. Washington Irving said that a southern lady who arrived with her costume exhibiting the profits of a rice plantation might meet a competitor from Salem, wrapped in the net proceeds of a cargo of whale oil. Other resorts with medicinal springs grew up, although White Sulphur Springs, Virginia, as late as 1817 was considered a little backwoodsy.

Music, with humorous or sentimental words that could be sung to well-known melodies, was popular in an era when entertainment in the home had to be provided by the family and guests for their own amusement. "The Blue Bell of Scotland," published in 1800 was typical, as was "Believe Me if All Those Endearing Young Charms" (1808) and " 'Tis the Last Rose of Summer" (1813), the last two having words by Thomas Moore, the Irish poet. Samuel Woodworth (1785–1842), author and newspaper editor, in 1818 wrote the popular "Old Oaken Bucket," which was put to music. Woodworth was also the author of one novel, in 1816, which, with the War of 1812 as the background, included the spirit of George Washington to guide America's latter-day generals. His play, *The Forest Rose*, first produced in 1825, was immensely popular for years. Collections of songs were brought out in books, sometimes pocket-size, with titles such as *The Forget Me Not Songster* and the *Museum of Mirth*. The editor of the latter assured his public that he had "expurgated every line of doubtful propriety."

A nation as much on the move as America, and with slow transportation that required many stopovers at night, needed inns and taverns. There were plenty of them, some quite good, or at least neat and clean. Others, especially as one traveled west, were shabby and dirty. Two or more beds to a room was the rule, and two persons to a bed—strangers or not. The presence of bedbugs was a regular complaint of travelers. At the same time, the inns and taverns were the meeting places where local affairs were talked over and where travelers from far places brought news to the local citizens. The taproom was a friendly place with good conversation, games and, not infrequently, heavy drinking. One inn in Lexington, Kentucky, in 1807 included a coffee house where forty-two different newspapers from all over the country could be read. Billiards, chess and backgammon were available, as well as native bourbon whiskey and imported French wines. While taverns little better than huts existed on the frontier, sizable hotels were built in the cities. The Exchange Coffee House, seven stories high, was begun in Boston in 1804.

Two other notable institutions of the time were the country stores and the itinerant peddlers, usually called Yankee peddlers since many of them originally came from New England. Most communities were too small to support a number of retail stores, each specializing in one line of goods. The result was the country store which, almost literally, carried a little of everything—food, clothing, farm equipment, housewares, and so on—that the particular community might want. Jedediah Barber opened his "Great Western Store" in Homer, New York, in 1813 in one moderate-sized room. It grew to three stories, plus an attic and a cellar, all jammed with goods of one variety or another. Much of such a storekeeper's trade was based on barter. He accepted farm products for his goods and then resold them, making a profit on both parts of the transaction. As a result, a country-store proprietor was likely to become an important businessman in his community, and he often added real-estate dealing and banking to storekeeping.

The Yankee peddler on his rounds was greeted with both pleasure and suspicion. He was a welcome visitor to lonely farm wives who seldom had anyone to talk to, but he earned a reputation as a slick dealer and a swindler. The peddler might have only such goods as he could carry on his back, but if he prospered he graduated to horseback, and then to horse and wagon. He is remembered particularly for the tinware he peddled, but he also carried a variety of items, especially ribbons, needles and combs which would find favor with the women.

The expanding service of the Post Office Department played a part in holding together the expanding country. There were 903 post offices in 1800, mail was carried over 20,817 miles of post roads and the clerks in the general office in Washington numbered seven. Twenty-five years later, there were 5,677 post offices, 94,052 miles of post roads and 27 clerks. The number of letters carried in 1801 was estimated at 2,240,000, or about one letter per adult. The total was up to nearly 9,000,000 by 1820. In the late 1820's nearly 27,000 employees, including postmasters, clerks and the drivers of the horses, were handling the mail. They used 2,879 carriages of different kinds and 17,584 horses. Some mail was still carried on horseback because of the condition of the roads. Congress as early as 1813 authorized the postmaster to use steamboats to transport mail, and in 1825 approved personal delivery of letters by carriers in the cities. The carrier collected two cents and the postmaster one cent for this extra service. The lowest rate for a letter in 1800 was eight cents and the smallest charge for carrying a piece of mail more than 100 miles was 12.5 cents. The mail service was not without its perils. The postmaster general was much pleased in 1806 when he found "two faithful, enterprising, hardy young woodsmen" who were willing to carry the mail from Cleveland to Detroit, which involved crossing the Great Black Swamp. Robbery of the mails was fairly common, so much so that Jefferson in 1808 was upset by "so frequent and great an evil." Most mail robbers were caught, and one was executed in 1825.

Newspapers, which often depended on the mails for distribution, also played a part in binding the nation, carrying as they did news from abroad as well as from all sections of the country. The newspapers of the time took an active role in politics. They devoted much space to the subject and almost all papers were strongly—even harshly and vindictively—partisan. The 150 or so American newspapers in 1800 grew to 863 in 1830, aided both by population growth and by improvements in printing presses. While the largest and most influential papers were in the eastern cities, newspapers followed the pioneers west. By the 1820's, for example, Cincinnati had two dailies, seven weeklies, a literary monthly, a medical journal and a magazine for teenagers. One of the papers, *Liberty Hall,* began with only 150 subscribers in 1804, but by 1813 circulation reached 2,000 a week. The most competent newspaper editor of the day was Hezekiah Niles (1777–1839), who founded *Niles' Weekly Register* in 1811 in Baltimore. In a time when much editorial writing consisted of vicious and unsupported attacks on the honesty and morality of individuals (including even George Washington), Niles kept his paper remarkably unbiased. It had a higher reputation both at home and abroad than any other paper of the period.

Many organizations which hoped to bring about one reform or another were active. Religious zeal, stemming from the Puritan inheritance and amplified by the Great Revival, directed the efforts of some groups toward ending what they considered personal sin and immorality—Sabbath-breaking, drinking, profanity, gambling and horse racing. Other persons and organizations, spurred by humanitarian feelings, were more concerned with poverty and juvenile delinquency and with charity for widows, orphans and the unemployed.

The Connecticut Society for the Reformation of Morals was formed in 1813, and was an active statewide organization. The first temperance society—aimed at reducing the amount of liquor consumed—was formed in New York State in 1808, and in 1812 the Presbyterian general assembly in Philadelphia appointed a committee to look into ways to restrict the use of alcohol. About that time it was estimated that there were at least 14,000 distilleries in the country, the number being so large because in rural areas many homes had their own distillery.

Reform movements of a humanitarian kind began in the cities

where the need was greatest. Church organizations also participated in this work, and such alleviation of social ills as took place was by private effort rather than through city governments. Most people involved in this work blamed individual laziness, intemperance and gambling for the problems of the poor, rather than any defects in the social order. In Boston a group of women established a Female Asylum in 1803, while in New York in 1806 another group set up the Orphan Asylum Society. Attempts were made at penal reform, and juvenile delinquency received attention. The latter was increasing, but whether at a faster rate than the population no one knew. The two remedies usually prescribed were new restrictions on delinquents and better instruction in useful trades.

Among individual reform leaders were Lucretia Mott (1793–1880) and Frances Wright (1795–1852). From 1818 on, Mrs. Mott, a Quaker born in Massachusetts, lectured on temperance, peace and the rights of labor. Later, in 1848, she was one of the organizers of the first woman's rights convention in the United States. Her husband, James Mott (1788–1868) was also a reformer who spent his life working for the abolition of slavery and for woman's suffrage. Miss Wright was born in Scotland, first visited the United States in 1818–20 and wrote an enthusiastic book about it which was published in 1821. She helped found the ill-fated Nashoba Community in 1824. Fanny Wright shocked conservatives by speaking on equal rights and birth control, and by addressing gatherings of workingmen. In keeping with the language newspaper editors of the time used, she was denounced as a "bold blasphemer and voluptuous preacher of licentiousness."

The most interesting experiment in communal living was that of New Harmony, Indiana, founded in 1825 by Robert Owen (1771–1858). He was a British reformer who, starting as a poor boy, had made a fortune as a cotton manufacturer in England and Scotland. He built one of the first model company towns, Lanark, Scotland, for his employees. In the New Harmony venture, which he took over from the George Rapp group, he was assisted by his son, Robert Dale Owen (1801–77). New Harmony attracted 1,000 or more settlers, who were to live together in complete equality of property and opportunity. Everyone would do his share of work and would have time to rest, play, study and meditate. Owen went to Washington to explain his plan to an interested audience that included both James Monroe and John Quincy Adams. William Maclure joined the venture, hoping to start an agricultural school. As seems to be true of most such projects, good intentions were not enough. New Harmony, which lasted little more than two years, was the victim of lack of direction and of dissension among those who were supposed to cooperate.

As the population grew, so did the cities, and at a faster rate. Only 6.1 per cent of the population lived in communities of 2,500 or more people in 1800; by 1820 the figure was 7.2 per cent; and by 1830, 8.8 per cent. This represented growth in the size of most of the older eastern cities and also the population in the new cities in the West. The United States nevertheless remained a rural nation and the Jeffersonian school of thought wanted it that way. Keeping in mind the experience of Europe, some Americans feared the lower classes of the cities who on occasion turned into mobs. On the other hand, most Americans equated material growth with progress, and it was plain that manufacturing, foreign trade, banking and transportation—and even a lively intellectual life—made it necessary for large numbers of different kinds of people to come together in cities. Western agrarian interests sometimes condemned the eastern cities as a source of evil, and yet the pioneers pushing west were as busy clearing city building sites as they were clearing farmland. Jefferson was torn. He saw that cities were important, even to "nourish some of the elegant arts," but he wondered, somewhat hopefully, in writing to Benjamin Rush in 1800 if perhaps the yellow fever epidemics might not discourage the growth of cities.

New York took first place in population in 1820, and by 1830 had 202,000 inhabitants. Philadelphia was second with 161,000, followed by Baltimore, 81,000; Boston, 61,000; New Orleans, 46,000; and Charleston, 30,000. After the Louisiana Purchase and the invention of the steamboat, New Orleans prospered and in the 1820's was the country's second-largest exporting city. The final important factor in the superiority achieved by New York City was the opening of the Erie Canal in the fall of 1825. At that time, De Witt Clinton, the "father" of the canal, predicted that within a century "the whole island of Manhattan, covered with habitations and replenished with a dense population, will constitute one vast city." In fact, the city in 1820 was built up as far north as Fourteenth Street.

Foreign visitors found American cities more pleasant than those of Europe. They thought them bright and airy and commented on the absence of run-down districts such as those in European cities. Fanny Wright, in her usual flamboyant manner, wrote of New York in 1821:

> No dark alleys. . . . no hovels, in whose ruined garrets, or dank and gloomy cellars crowd the wretched victims of vice and leisure, whose penury drives to despair, ere she opens them to the grave.

Miss Wright was too optimistic. A slum area began to develop on the city's lower east side as early as 1815, and Boston had its areas of urban poor. The formation of the New York Society for the Prevention of Pauperism in 1817 and similar organizations in other cities indicate that the problem of urban poverty already existed.

Municipalities were starting to assume more responsibility for police and fire protection, water supply and public health in the early nineteenth century. New York had a board of health in 1805 and Philadelphia in 1818, but neither had any regular staff and they did little except when the emergency of an epidemic arose. Quarantine measures were then enforced. Only eighteen small waterworks systems existed in 1800, and only one of these was city owned. The privately controlled Manhattan Company in 1799 operated a system in New York, collecting water in a reservoir and supplying it through hollow logs. As time went on the water became contaminated, but an adequate municipal system was not completed until 1842. Philadelphia's water-supply system, completed in 1801 on the basis of plans submitted by Benjamin Henry Latrobe, was the pride of the city. Pure water was brought to a reservoir in Center Square where a pumping station distributed it throughout the city by means of hollowed-out log pipes. Latrobe designed and constructed a handsome Greek temple to house the steam pump and hide its utilitarian looks.

In addition to convenience and health, more adequate water supplies were badly needed for fire fighting as cities grew larger and buildings were crowded together. For many years, fire fighting was a matter of volunteer companies. The firemen used leather buckets and formed bucket brigades to pass the water. Hand pumpers with lengths of leather hose were in use by 1800. Philadelphia was the first city to devise a system for connecting hoses to hydrants to fill the pumpers instead of relying on bucket brigades.

Police protection became professionalized sooner than fire fighting, but was not highly organized. Uniforms were not worn and patrols were usually out only at night. Philadelphia in 1803 had fourteen constables, one for each ward, and a chief constable. New York, around 1802, could boast of the first detective. He was one Jacob Hays, who specialized in disguises. The usual crimes of robbery and assault were common to all cities, but in 1805 Cincinnati rounded up a gang of horse thieves.

One American historian said, "The towns were the spearheads of the frontier." Towns were started ahead of the line of farming settlement and their growth, which was rapid at times, was an important factor in the opening up of the West. All the midwest cities that were to rise to prominence were already established by 1820 except Chicago, Milwaukee and Indianapolis. The boosters and promoters who founded towns and dealt in real estate expected their communities would become metropolises. Many, of course, never got past the stage of being small villages, and withered away as transportation routes passed them by.

Pittsburgh was the oldest of the frontier cities east of the Mississippi. While its population in 1800 was only 1,565, in fifteen years it grew to 8,000. By then, too, Pittsburgh was becoming a leading manufacturing city, but up to 1806 it had only one paved street. Cincinnati, on down the Ohio, was a rival of Pittsburgh for the trade of the West. It had a population of 750 in 1800, which rose to about 5,000 in 1815, making it the largest city in Ohio. Cincinnati boasted a mill with a seventy-horsepower steam engine, designed by Oliver Evans, that could grind 700 barrels of flour a week. There were also three Protestant churches, a Quaker meetinghouse and three banks.

Cincinnati's most prominent citizen was Daniel Drake (1785–1852), a physician by training, a civic leader by nature. He founded the Medical College of Ohio (1819) and the Commercial Hospital and Lunatic Asylum (1821). Drake also helped establish a lyceum, a circulating library, a seminary and a museum, and was a director of a bank. He made a pioneering study of disease in relation to geography, wrote a book boosting the virtues of Cincinnati, and in his drugstore introduced soda water to the people of his city. Drake was the nineteenth-century type of self-made man who, given the conditions of a newly settled area, could turn his hand to developing every aspect of it. No wonder he was called the "Franklin of the West."

Cleveland, although founded officially as early as 1796 when Moses Cleaveland had a city plan laid out, fell far behind Pittsburgh and Cincinnati. It consisted of only 150 people and two streets in 1815. A little later, a road connecting it to the Ohio River and the introduction of steamboats to the Great Lakes spurred Cleveland's growth. Louisville's establishment goes as far back as 1778, but in 1800 there were only 359 inhabitants. Louisville's importance stemmed from the fact that it was located at the one point on the Ohio where falls made it necessary to transship goods. By 1815 Louisville had a population of 2,700 and one of the most advanced police systems in the West. The police, however, were more for the control of slaves than anything else. Louisville was one of the first western cities to install street lighting, but unfortunately there and elsewhere breaking lamps was a favorite recreation of some teenagers.

Lexington, Kentucky, named for the town in Massachusetts where the first battle of the Revolution took place, was the only western city of importance not on navigable water. At the start of the century it prospered because it had good land connections, but the coming of the steamboat relegated it to second-rate status. The population of Lexington in 1800, which was 1,795, exceeded that of Pittsburgh. Lexington in its heyday was a cultural center, too, as it was the home of Transylvania University, the first such institution west of the mountains. St. Louis, Missouri, whose history went back to the days of French rule, had about 1,000 inhabitants, of whom a quarter were slaves, in 1804 when the United States took over. St. Louis was largely dependent on the fur trade and had a reputation for being a dangerous town because hostile Indians remained in the area, which except for the city was largely unsettled. St. Louis's reputation and population went up after troops were sent there during the War of 1812.

In the history of any nation, in any particular period of time, unique events occur, unusual people attract attention, nature misbehaves. The possibilities are endless. Some of these "happenings" are important, some are not, but a nation's life would be dull without them.

One pleasant and sentimental happening took place between August, 1824, and September, 1825, when the Marquis de Lafayette visited the United States. In 1777, when he was only nineteen, the marquis had left his high and comfortable position in France to offer his military services to the colonies in their fight for independence. Created a major general at once, he fought valiantly, being wounded at Brandywine, suffering with Washington in the winter at Valley Forge and taking part in the final battle at Yorktown. He returned to France, still under thirty, where he remained and where his fortunes went up and down during the French Revolution. Now, at the age of sixty-seven, he was back to visit the scenes of his greatest adventure. He was enthusiastically welcomed by the people. In October, 1824, General Lafayette, the last surviving general officer to serve with Washington, met James Monroe, the last United States president who had fought in the Revolution. Congress voted him $200,000, since the general was now a poor man, and a whole township of land near Tallahassee, Florida.

Quite a different type of person was John Chapman (1774-1845), born in Massachusetts and better known as Johnny Appleseed. He began his wanderings in western Pennsylvania, Ohio and Indiana about 1800, planting appleseeds as he went. For forty years he traveled, planting and caring for his trees, becoming a familiar sight everywhere with his ragged clothes and eccentric manners. During the War of 1812 he saved the people of Mansfield, Ohio, by swiftly going thirty miles to summon American troops who forestalled an Indian attack.

Two events that somehow seem typically American involved an enormous cheese and the origin of the nickname "Uncle Sam." On New Year's Day, 1802, President Jefferson was presented with a cheese more than four feet in diameter, fifteen inches thick and weighing 1,235 pounds. It had been made the previous summer by Elder John Leland's congregation in Cheshire, Massachusetts, and the story has it that the cheese required the milk of 900 cows. Leland and a companion conveyed it to Washington by wagon and boat, and when they presented it to Jefferson he commented sagely that it was certainly unusual proof of skill in the domestic arts. Within a day about sixty pounds had to be removed from the middle because of signs of decay. No one knows what eventually happened to the cheese. Some said the last of it was served at a presidential reception in 1805, but others said it had long since been dumped in the Potomac River.

Uncle Sam, as a term to designate the United States government, came into use during the War of 1812. It was used at that time as a term of derision by those opposing the war, but it later became a general term, widely used. No absolute proof has turned up as to its origin. "Uncle Sam" probably derived simply from the "U.S." on army uniforms and other government property. A more interesting possibility concerns Samuel Wilson (1766–1854) of Troy, New York. Known to his friends as Uncle Sam, he was an inspector of army supplies and supposedly stamped "U.S." on goods he approved. In any event, the term first appeared in print in the Troy *Post*, September 7, 1813.

The year 1811 was full of signs that encouraged people to believe the Second Coming and the Millennium were at hand. In the spring there were heavy floods; squirrels by the thousands headed south, many of them drowning while attempting to cross the Ohio River; a comet appeared; and in the fall, when the first steamboat was navigating the Mississippi River, the whole valley was shaken by earthquakes. To add a final touch of doom, on Christmas night the Richmond Theater burned with a loss of more than sixty lives, including the governor of the state of Virginia. The Monumental Church of Richmond, so-called because it was a memorial to the fire victims, was erected on the spot (1811–14) and was designed by Robert Mills.

Life in America, then as always, consisted of the important and the inconsequential, the good and the bad, the planned and the unexpected.

16   The Character of America in 1825

THE UNITED STATES OF AMERICA was a considerably different country in 1825 from what it had been in 1800. Physically and materially it had grown in ways no one in 1800 could have imagined. Its territory was doubled as a result of the Louisiana Purchase so that, with the right to joint occupation of the Oregon Territory, the United States now extended from the Atlantic to the Pacific. At the same time, while its farmlands spread westward and increased every day, America was also a manufacturing nation and becoming more so all the time. What had been a small nation on the Eastern seaboard, was well on its way to conquering the better part of a continent.

The increase of population kept pace with territorial expansion. By 1825 the United States counted about 11,250,000 people, more than double the number in 1800. About 2,000,000 of the total were Blacks, mostly slaves in the South. The part of the population living west of the Allegheny Mountains had increased to 27 per cent by 1820, or more than 2,500,000, further evidence of the country's ability to settle a continent.

While every American was an immigrant or a descendant of an immigrant, newcomers in the period 1800 to 1825 did not play a great part. No records were kept until 1820 but the number of immigrants from 1800 to 1815 was low because the constant turmoil of the Napoleonic Wars in Europe made it difficult if not impossible for people to come to America. After 1815 the flow of immigration increased considerably, and did not let up for a hundred years. The best estimate accounts for about 250,000 immigrants in the quarter century. Great Britain and Germany contributed the most, as they had before, but toward the end of the period the number arriving from Ireland increased noticeably.

The twenty-five-year period witnessed political and diplomatic changes, too. One gets the impression that around 1800 the nation and its leaders were looking forward to a period in which America could go its own way. It had been free of Great Britain long enough to feel unshackled, its Federal government under the Constitution had run quite smoothly for a dozen years, its attitude toward Europe was to ignore it as much as possible. Yet the quarter century turned out to be a disturbing one, both domestically and in foreign affairs.

At home the snarled election of 1800 was a rude shock and one that affected party politics from then on, in spite of the brief Era of Good Feelings. The election showed up a flaw in the Constitution and revealed the depth of political partisanship. Toward the end of the era, the clash between North and South, between slave and free states, resulting in the Missouri Compromise, was another shock to those who expected smooth political sailing for the government in Washington. The Compromise uncovered political, economic and ethical conflict that only the blindest could think was settled for good in 1820.

In foreign affairs the United States was unwillingly caught up in the life-and-death struggle between Great Britain and France that did not end until 1815. The question of what America's policy toward warring Europe should be brought tumult to domestic politics, caused economic problems and, finally, put the nation at war again with Great Britain, barely a generation after the Revolution. This was a war America didn't intend to get into, one that it fought badly once in, and one that gained it nothing tangible in the end. Yet the fact of having stood off the British once more had lasting effects on the spirit and morale of the nation. Finally, the statement of the Monroe Doctrine in late 1823 was an indication that the nation felt able to defy the powers of Europe and to warn them not to meddle in the affairs of the New World.

The unity achieved by the Revolution, formed by the Constitution and the establishment of the Federal government, and cemented by the War of 1812 was expressed by 1825 in self-confidence and in a stronger feeling than ever that America was entirely different from Europe. People believed the path the country was to follow would keep it unique and safe from the evil ways into which Europe had fallen. Noah Webster in his spelling book expressed it:

> Europe is grown old in folly, corruption, and tyranny. . . . American glory begins at dawn at a favorable period, and under flattering circumstances.

One result of this feeling of difference was an outburst of national pride that found expression in many ways. This was apparent by 1825 in literature and other cultural areas where American subject matter by then predominated. Pride of country showed even more obviously in the universal celebration of July 4th, in enthusiasm for the flag and the American eagle, and in the observance of George Washington's birthday, which soon ranked second only to Independence Day. Congress in 1818 decided to limit the number of stripes in the flag to thirteen in honor of the founding states, while continuing to add a star for each new state.

Following logically after the nation's pride in what it had accomplished by 1825 was the almost universal belief that the United States was chosen by destiny to have an even more glorious future. On the more intellectual side, this optimism was based on faith in progress which would be assisted by cultural and scientific advances. A nation of America's resources, and freed from Europe's past, could chart its own path and that path must eventually lead to superiority in every realm. In the down-to-earth region of material things, America's uniqueness, combined with its great resources, must inevitably result in the spread of its own brand of civilization from coast to coast. A man who expressed this thought in the language of the day was Hugh Swinton Legaré (1797–1843), a statesman from South Carolina, a strong believer in America's destiny, but more philosophic about it than some. He held various positions, eventually becoming secretary of state only two months before his death. In a speech at an Independence Day celebration in 1823, he said:

> . . . at no distant day, the language of Milton shall be spoken from shore to shore, over the vastest portion of the earth's surface that was ever inhabited by a race worthy of speaking a language consecrated to liberty.

The "Virginia Dynasty"—Jefferson, Madison and Monroe—and the men who assisted them gave the nation excellent leadership in a difficult quarter of a century. But when the era is looked at as a whole, when all its best men are assessed, one man stands out: Thomas Jefferson. If America was unique among nations, Jefferson was unique among men of his time. His intelligence and talents were so great and so varied that no part of the life of the country was untouched by them. A nation that possessed a Thomas Jefferson was entitled to look with confidence to the future, even if his political enemies of the time could not see him as history must see him today —a symbol of his era.

Reading List

ADAMS, HENRY. *History of the United States during the Administrations of Jefferson and Madison.* Abridged. Englewood Cliffs: Prentice-Hall, Inc., 1963. Paper.

————. *The United States in 1800.* Ithaca: Cornell University Press, 1955. Paper.

BAKELESS, JOHN (ed.). *The Journals of Lewis and Clark: A New Selection.* New York: New American Library, Inc., 1964. Paper.

BERGMAN, PETER M. *The Chronological History of the Negro in America.* New York: New American Library, Inc., 1969. Paper.

BERKY, ANDREW S., and SHENTON, JAMES P. (eds.). *The Historians' History of the United States.* Vol. I. New York: Capricorn Books, 1966. Paper.

BILLINGTON, RAY ALLEN. *The Westward Movement in the United States.* New York: Van Nostrand-Reinhold Books, 1959. Paper.

BOORSTIN, DANIEL J. *The Americans: The National Experience.* New York: Random House, Inc., 1965.

BRANT, IRVING. *The Fourth President: A Life of James Madison.* Indianapolis: The Bobbs-Merrill Co., Inc., 1970.

BROOKS, VAN WYCK. *The World of Washington Irving.* New York: E. P. Dutton & Co., Inc., 1944.

BURCHARD, JOHN, and BUSH-BROWN, ALBERT. *The Architecture of America: A Social and Cultural History.* Abridged ed. Boston: Little, Brown & Co., 1967.

COLES, HARRY L. *The War of 1812.* Chicago: University of Chicago Press, 1965. Paper.

COLLIER, JOHN. *Indians of the Americas.* New York: New American Library, Inc., 1947. Paper.

CONDIT, CARL W. *American Building Art: The Nineteenth Century.* New York: Oxford University Press, Inc., 1960.

CRESSON, W. P. *James Monroe*. Chapel Hill: University of North Carolina Press, 1946.

CUNLIFFE, MARCUS. *The Literature of the United States*. Baltimore: Penguin Books, 1961. Paper.

———. *The Nation Takes Shape: 1789–1837*. Chicago: University of Chicago Press, 1959. Paper.

CURTI, MERLE. *The Growth of American Thought*. 3rd ed. New York: Harper & Row, Publishers, 1964.

DANGERFIELD, GEORGE. *The Awakening of American Nationalism: 1815–1828*. New York: Harper & Row, Publishers, 1965. Paper.

———. *The Era of Good Feelings*. New York: Harcourt, Brace & World, Inc., 1952.

DAVIDSON, MARSHALL B. *The American Heritage History of Notable American Houses*. New York: American Heritage Publishing Co., Inc., 1971.

DEVOTO, BERNARD. *Across the Wide Missouri*. Boston: Houghton Mifflin Co., 1947.

DULLES, FOSTER RHEA. *A History of Recreation: America Learns to Play*. 2nd ed. New York: Appleton-Century-Crofts, 1965.

———. *Labor in America*. 3rd ed. New York: Thomas Y. Crowell Co., 1966.

EATON, CLEMENT. *The Growth of Southern Civilization: 1790–1860*. New York: Harper & Row, Publishers, 1961.

FAULKNER, HAROLD U. *American Economic History*. 8th ed. New York: Harper & Row, Publishers, 1960.

FEHRENBACHER, DON E. *The Era of Expansion: 1800–1848*. New York: John Wiley & Sons, Inc., 1969.

FRANKLIN, JOHN HOPE. *From Slavery to Freedom: A History of Negro Americans*. 3rd ed. New York: Alfred A. Knopf, Inc., 1967.

GLAAB, CHARLES N., and BROWN, A. THEODORE. *A History of Urban America*. New York: The Macmillan Co., 1967.

GREEN, CONSTANCE M., *Washington: Village and Capital, 1800–1878*. Princeton: Princeton University Press, 1962.

GRUVER, REBECCA BROOKS. *American Nationalism, 1783–1830: A Self-Portrait*. New York: Capricorn Books, 1970. Paper.

HAGAN, WILLIAM T. *American Indians*. Chicago: University of Chicago Press, 1961.

JOSEPHY, ALVIN M., JR. *The Indian Heritage of America*. New York: Alfred A. Knopf, Inc., 1968.

KROUT, JOHN ALLEN, and FOX, DIXON RYAN. *The Completion of Independence: 1790–1830.* New York: The Macmillan Co., 1944.

LARKIN, OLIVER W. *Art and Life in America.* Rev. ed. New York: Holt, Rinehart and Winston, Inc., 1960.

MALONE, DUMAS. *Jefferson the President: First Term, 1801–1805.* Boston: Little, Brown & Co., 1970.

———. *Jefferson the President: Second Term, 1805–1809.* Boston: Little, Brown & Co., 1974.

NYE, RUSSEL BLAINE. *The Cultural Life of the New Nation: 1776–1830.* New York: Harper & Row, Publishers, 1960.

PETERSON, MERRILL D. *Thomas Jefferson and the New Nation.* New York: Oxford University Press, Inc., 1970.

PHILBRICK, FRANCIS S. *The Rise of the West: 1754–1830.* New York: Harper & Row, Publishers, 1965.

PRATT, JULIUS W. *Expansionists of 1812.* Gloucester: Peter Smith, 1925.

SABLOSKY, IRVING. *American Music.* Chicago: University of Chicago Press, 1969.

SANFORD, CHARLES L. (ed.). *Quest for America: 1810–1824.* Garden City: Doubleday & Co., Inc., 1964. Paper.

SCHACHNER, NATHAN. *Aaron Burr: A Biography.* New York: Frederick A. Stokes Co., 1937.

SPILLER, ROBERT E. (ed.). *The American Literary Revolution: 1783–1837.* Garden City: Doubleday & Co., Inc., 1967.

STAMPP, KENNETH M. *The Peculiar Institution: Slavery in the Ante-Bellum South.* New York: Alfred A. Knopf, Inc., 1956.

TAYLOR, WILLIAM R. *Cavalier and Yankee.* New York: George Braziller, Inc., 1961.

TURNER, FREDERICK JACKSON. *The Frontier in American History.* New York: Holt, Rinehart and Winston, Inc., 1920.

WADE, RICHARD C. *The Urban Frontier: Pioneer Life in Early Pittsburgh, Cincinnati, Lexington, Louisville, and St. Louis.* Cambridge: Harvard University Press, 1959.

WALTERS, RAYMOND, JR. *Albert Gallatin: Jeffersonian Financier and Diplomat.* New York: The Macmillan Co., 1957.

———. *The Virginia Dynasty: The United States, 1801–1829.* New York: Van Nostrand-Reinhold Books, 1965. Paper.

WEINSTEIN, ALLEN, and GATELL, FRANK OTTO (eds.). *American Negro Slavery: A Modern Reader.* 2nd ed. New York: Oxford University Press, Inc., 1973.

WHITE, LEONARD D. *The Jeffersonians: A Study in Administrative History, 1801–1829.* New York: The Macmillan Co., 1951.

WILTSE, CHARLES M. *The New Nation: 1800–1845.* New York: Hill and Wang, 1961.

WISSLER, CLARK. *Indians of the United States.* Rev. ed. Garden City: Doubleday & Co., Inc., 1966.

WORCESTER, DONALD E., and SCHAEFFER, WENDELL G. *The Growth and Culture of Latin America.* Vol. I: From Conquest to Independence. 2nd ed. New York: Oxford University Press, Inc., 1970.

WRIGHT, LOUIS B. *Culture on the Moving Frontier.* Bloomington: Indiana University Press, 1955.

Index

WITHDRAWN FROM
KENT STATE UNIVERSITY LIBRARIES